How to Master Breathwork

Learn How to Master Your Breath to Conquer Anxiety, Manage Your Anger and Improve Your Physical Health

Author: Piia Rauha

Free Gift

This book includes a bonus booklet. This giveaway may be for a limited time only. All information on how you can secure your gift right now can be found at the end of this book.

Table Of Contents

CHAPTER 4 BREATHWORK FOR ANGER MANAGEMENT
....49

CHAPTER 5 BREATHWORK FOR CHRONIC PAIN 67

CHAPTER 6 BREATHWORK FOR TRAUMA.....................77

Go from Stress to Success with These 15 Powerful Tips

You're in The Tunnel, Now Turn on The Light:

Here are The Best Ways to Transform Your Success

Do You Feel Stressed-Out, Overwhelmed and Harassed Every Day?

Then you're stuck in a negative thought spiral that is keeping you from achieving *real success!*

How many times have you thought, 'if only I could be more productive, then I'd get ahead?' No matter how hard you try, it eludes you. Most people experience intense self-doubt, worry and negative thinking at some point in their careers. These are your immediate obstacles to success.

This guide tackles these issues with easy, direct solutions to help you break the cycle and get back on track. These 15 powerful tips will take you from overwhelmed to overjoyed, in no time!

This FREE Cheat Sheet contains:

- Essential tips on how to stop worrying and start living

- How to actually relieve anxiety and banish it for good

- Ways to get rid of negative thoughts, and how to stop them from recurring

- Tips to become the most productive, motivated version of yourself

- How to focus on career success and build positive cycles and habits

Scroll down and <u>click the link</u> below to Claim your Free Cheat Sheet!

I want you to know that you don't have to live this way. You don't have to feel like these negative cycles are getting the better of you. Your career is waiting to bloom – and flourish! Give yourself the opportunity to make the right choices, by learning how to authentically reach for lasting success.

Ditch the stress, embrace success.

<u>Click Here!</u>

Book Description:

Breathing is something that we human beings take for granted, but inhales and exhales are more than just a means of getting air. Breathing fortifies us with much-needed oxygen to continue living. Still, it is also a way to help us manage stressful life situations and medical conditions such as PTSD, anxiety, and chronic pain.

Breathing in the right way can enhance your quality of life, reduce stress, help balance your emotions, and heal your body from the inside out. Our ancestors saw the power breathing bestows and incorporated it into meditation, yoga, and Tai Chi practices that we can now benefit from in the modern world. Breathing clean is known as breathwork, and when done correctly, we can live happier, calmer, more comfortable lives.

This easy-to-read guidebook will educate you on:

- An in-depth explanation about breathwork and how it works
- The benefits of breathwork and long-term implications
- The different techniques you can use to practice breathwork
- How you can use breathwork to reduce anxiety and manage your anger
- How you can use breathwork to manage chronic pain
- How you can use breathwork to cope with PTSD and other trauma
- So much more!

It is time to open up your mind and see the real possibilities that changing the way you breathe can have on your life. Read more to become transcended!

Introduction

Breathing.

It is a process that we as humans take for granted. It is an unconscious phenomenon that we count on to continue living, yet we often forget it is happening and that we have some measure of control on how it happens.

Breathing is when we take in air into our lungs and expel it out back into the world. It sounds like such a simple, cut-and-dry process, doesn't it? But what if it meant more? What if, through the power of inhalation and exhalation, you can connect more deeply with the universe to center yourself and gain a sense of direction? What if you could use breathing to help you get through life's difficult situations? Exhaling away anxiety and anger while breathing in positivity and the courage to keep on going on even when life seems too tough. What if you could use the power of breathing to push away the trauma and also help heal your body physically?

What if these questions were not hypothetical but instead possible?

This book was created to help you understand the power of inhalation, exhalation, and how you can use that power to enhance the quality of your life. By reducing stress, anxiety, balancing your emotions, increasing concentration, and focus you will heal your body from the inside out. This power is called breathwork, and it is a conscious breathing technique that helps you control your mental, spiritual, emotional, and physical world.

Breathing is more than just taking in air. It tells us when things are going right and when something is wrong with our body as well as our mind. Think about it... Often the first sign of injury, disease, or mental distress is short or shallow breathing. This is a symptom that we need to pay attention to and is often the first indication that allows us to take action. Similarly, breathing that is too fast can also mean that something is wrong and we need to pay attention so it can be rectified.

When we are most happy, calm, and uncomfortable, our breaths are measured and balanced. It is not erratic and fast, nor is it too shallow. It has just that right pitch. You can control the pitch so you live life with a calm mind, a light heart, and your body is working at its optimal performance. That is the power of breathing and breathwork. It puts the control back in your hands through simple techniques that anyone can practice from the comfort of their homes.

What You Will Learn From This Book

This book is full of helpful information that will give you insight into the technique of breathwork and how it can be useful in your life. These pages contain:

- An in-depth explanation of breathwork and how it works.
- The many benefits of breathwork.
- The different techniques you can use to practice breathwork.
- How you can use breathwork to reduce anxiety and manage anger.
- How you can use breathwork to manage chronic pain.
- How you can use breathwork to cope with trauma.
- And so much more.

Before we move further, I would like to take the time to thank you for downloading this book. My hope is that you gain the highest value from it and that you can use the techniques and advice contained within these pages to enhance your life and benefit from the power of the practice. Read this book with an open mind so you can easily transcend to a state of being where you are not merely existing or controlled by outside forces. Realize that you are the one in the driver's seat of life, and this control was given to you through the power of your God-given right to breathe.

This book comes with a FREE Bonus chapter section as a gift. You can download them for free. The free content can be found at the bottom of this book.

Chapter 1
What is Breathwork?

"If you want to conquer the anxiety of life, live in the moment, live in the breath."

— *Amit Ray*

Breathwork is a combination of exercises and techniques that are performed to help a person improve their mental, physical, spiritual, and emotional capacity. Rather than unconsciously inhaling and exhaling, breathwork involves the deliberate change of your breathing pattern in a systematic way meant to promote deep relaxation. This leaves a person feeling energized and focused.

Practices that aid with the development of self-awareness like yoga and meditation are based on controlling your breath with awareness and intent. Breathwork is not a new practice. It has been around since ancient times and has evolved to include new techniques that are a means of self-healing and therapy. Breathwork practices and procedures usually involve a few minutes to an hour of sustained rhythmic breathing. Typically, practitioners of breathwork report increased feelings of clarity and alertness during and afterward.

Typically, people think of breathwork as the physical aspect of breathing where the inhale and exhale of air occurs. Of course, this is a vital part of living as inhaling brings much-needed oxygen into the body. This oxygen is taken into the lungs and delivered to the blood vessel where it is then passed to other organs in the body. These organs use oxygen to keep the body working right and thriving. Oxygen is needed for metabolism to occur, to rejuvenate the cells in the body and to ensure that the brain fires neural communication in a productive, efficient manner and many more processes.

Exhalation removes carbon dioxide from the body. Carbon dioxide is a waste product and if it develops into too high a level inside of our bodies, it slowly poisons us. This release of carbon dioxide is vital to maintaining the world that we live in because trees use it to manufacture their food. Trees expel oxygen as a waste product, so we actually come full circle with the creation, intake, and release of oxygen and carbon dioxide.

The physical aspect of breathwork takes a coordinated effort even if you are not aware of it. Your brain, chest, back and belly work to coordinate the simple yet seamless process. The effects of inhales and exhales are immediate. Your nervous system is activated and slows down the rate of your heart and lowers your blood pressure to help you feel calm. Your chest and neck muscles relax as your chest moves up and down to take in and expel air. This relaxed feeling is magnified as oxygen reaches your other body organs and cells.

When your body is in distress, such as a dangerous situation where your fight-or-flight response is activated, your breathing picks up,this comes as a response to the surge in the levels of adrenaline and cortisol. When your breath picks up so too does the rate of your pulse and blood pressure, putting your body in a state of hyper-vigilance. To reverse this state, you need to deepen and slow your breath so you can relax your body. As you do this, you will notice the rise and fall of your chest, belly, and the temperature and moisture of your breath. As you calm down and relax, you will notice how your body shifts away from shallow breathing to deep, measured breathing and how this affects your muscles and bones.

Breathwork is not only compiled of physical responses. It also helps calm your mind and slow down the emotional surges in your head. The effects are so extensive, allowing a person to access a deeper state of mind, that it can be used to help treat PTSD, depression, anger, and anxiety. With this access, the breathwork practitioner can study traumas of the past and present, emotions or grudges, to release themselves. To enter a deeper state of mind using breathwork, you need to be aware of the thoughts in your head and to be able to study them objectively. You also need to be mindful of your emotions and what your inner voice is saying. Visualize your intent while practicing breathwork.

Breathwork also allows you to connect with your true self and your spiritual being. For this to be effective, you need to disconnect with your ego and how you think things should be to connect with the universe so that a spiritual awakening can occur. This is a place where you let go of your limiting thoughts and allow possibilities to enter your mind. There you can enable the universe to sink in as you inhale and expel negative energy from your body as you exhale.

A Brief History of Breathwork

For centuries, human beings have used conscious breathing as a technique for self-healing, relaxation. and spiritual awakening. This was especially prominent in Eastern cultures, where Tai Chi and Buddhism emerged. In many of these traditional cultures, spirit and breath are synonymous. For example, in Latin, the word *spiritus* describes the physical intake of air as well as spirit. In India, the word *prana* means air and "sacred essence of life." In Chinese, the word for breath is *Chi*. It also means "universal and cosmic energy of life." Finally, in Greek, the word *pneuma* stands for both air and spirit since it is a sound belief in Greece that breath is connected to the mind and spirit.

This is not the only culture that believes in this connection. So many traditional cultures used breathwork techniques in spiritual and religious practices. The Essenes, a people of the Jewish sect who flourished in the 2nd century BCE to the 1st century CE, used to submerge people underwater to induce an experience of death and rebirth. This practice limited the intake of breath until the person was considered reborn. Then, of course, the person could breathe freely, a signal of their rebirth.

Shamanic cultures also used breathing techniques to foster a state of self-discovery, transformation, and healing. Traditional Indian yoga practice also utilized pranayama breathing, which is a practice that involves holding one's breath for prolonged periods and a hyperventilating-like style of breathing to help awaken the spiritual self and heal the body and mind. Also, the Kalahari '!Kung' Bushmen of Africa perform a ritual that involves dancing while performing rapid and shallow breathwork to attain '!kia', which is a state of emotional and physical ecstasy.

Breathwork extended far across the globe and many other cultural practices incorporated it. Such as, Siddha Yoga, a spiritual path founded by Muktananda from 1908-1982 that is based on Indian yogic philosophies. Sufi practices, a mystical Islam practice that emphasizes finding God internally and moving away from materialism. Kundalini Yoga, a style originating from the Shaktism and Tantra schools of Hinduism. As well as Taoist meditation a meditative practice of visualization, contemplation, mindfulness, and concentration. All of which are associated with Chinese philosophies and the Taoism religion.

The introduction of breathwork in the Western world came in the mid-1900s. Wilhelm Reich (1897-1957), who was a student of Sigmund Freud (1856-1939), the German neurologist who founded psychoanalysis, researched breathing techniques within psychology and psychiatry. Reich was a psychoanalyst who developed a therapy known as character analysis vegetotherapy. This type of treatment consisted of exploring repressed memories and releasing emotions stored in the body through the technique of breathwork. A student of his named Alexander Lowen developed this research and founded a technique called bioenergetics. Bioenergetics used breathwork along with different body postures and exercises to summon spiritual energy within an individual.

In the 1960s, Leonard Orr, who was born in 1949, developed rebirthing breathwork, while he was sitting in a hot tub and experimenting with deep breathing practices. He stated that he envisioned part of his birth during the experiment, and it allowed him to purge his system of repressed traumatic childhood memories. He has proposed that the rebirthing breathwork technique can relieve pain and cure diseases. He has since then gone onto creating several books on the subject and is a modern-day yogi and visionary among his many titles.

Since then other techniques have been developed, such as holotropic breathwork, which was developed by Stanislav Grof, psychiatrist, and his late wife, Christina Grof in the 1970s. The holotropic breathwork technique was developed as a means for self-exploration, personal empowerment and personal enlightenment by controlling someone's breathing patterns. The word holotropic was derived from the two Greek words *holos*, which means whole and *trepein*, which means move toward. Translated, the word holotropic means moving toward wholeness.

Since the 1970s, there have been many breakthroughs in the field of breathwork therapy. Such breakthroughs include the founding of integrative breathwork by Jacquelyn Small in 1991. Small is well known for her work in areas of spiritual, psychology and personal transformation. She worked alongside Stanislav Grof to develop the integrative breathwork technique, which is a pattern of conscious breathing that induces safe and natural physical, emotional, mental, and spiritual healing.

The clarity breathwork technique, which is an evolved form of rebirthing breathwork technique was established in 1999, and the field of breathwork continues to develop every year. There are many certification programs available worldwide for people who are interested and would like to practice and become facilitators. Organizations like The Stanislav and Christina Grof Foundation, Rebirthing Breathwork International (RBI), The Global Professional Breathwork Alliance (GPBA), and The International Breathwork Foundation (IBF) are dedicated to expanding on the work of the pioneers in this field and continue to provide training and research as needed.

The Benefits of Breathwork

By taking just a few moments every day to practice conscious breathing, you do your body, mind, and spirit a world of good.

Breathwork helps you improve your overall well-being, and its benefits include:

- Aiding with the processing of emotions and dealing with emotional pain and trauma. We tend to get lost in our feelings especially when they are painful, but breathwork allows us to sort through these emotions and give us control so that we can choose how we deal with them rather than just going with the flow of how they move us.

- Increasing joy and happiness. Breathwork helps us stay grounded in the moment so that we enjoy these moments rather than just passing through them. This helps us feel more fulfilled and therefore, happy.

- Increasing self-image, self-confidence, and self-esteem through the process of allowing us to be more self-aware. Breathwork allows you to become more in touch with your emotions and thoughts and therefore, with who you are on a fundamental level. This increases your love for yourself and therefore, allows you to feel more capable in everyday situations.

- Reducing stress and anxiety levels. Again, becoming more in touch with your innermost thoughts and feelings allows you to breathe away negativity, inhale positivity so that you are happier and less stressed or anxious.

- Being a natural painkiller. Deep breathing promotes the release of endorphins, which are hormones that are fondly called feel-good hormones. They promote pain relief and elevated moods.

- Improving blood flow and circulation. The upward and downward movement of the diaphragm during breathwork removes toxins from the body, which allows for better blood flow and circulation.

- Improving posture. It is a little-known fact that position and breathing are related but breathing in deeply and consciously causes you to straighten up your spine in the process.

- Detoxifying the body. Carbon dioxide, which is the waste product that we expel during exhales, can build up in the body over time. This is especially prominent when we practice shallow breathing regularly. This buildup can lead to illness. Therefore, practicing measured, deep breathing can expel more of this toxic air from the system and detoxify our bodies. Breathwork also helps detoxify the body by allowing the lymphatic system to work more efficiently. The lymphatic system is a network of organs and tissues that help the body get rid of unwanted material such as waste and toxins. This process is facilitated by a liquid called lymph, which contains infection and disease-fighting white blood cells. Deep, measured breathing allows lymph to flow more efficiently hence detoxifying the body more efficiently.

- Reducing acidity in the body. Many cancers and the disease called chronic inflammation, which is the destruction of body cells over a prolonged period such as several months to years through an overreaction of immune defense, thrive in acidic bodies. Stress is a major cause of acidity levels rising in the body. Breathwork helps to reduce stress and thus makes the body more alkaline and better able to fight off these cancers and inflammation.

- Increasing energy levels. Deeper, measured breaths allow more oxygen to enter the bloodstream and as a result, increases energy levels.

- Aiding in beating addictions. Most addictions arise through the positive associations the brain makes with harmful things. By using breathwork, you can disassociate these destructive behaviors with emotions that make you feel good.

- Improving your professional and personal relationships. Breathwork allows you to think before you speak and act. This can play a significant role in enhancing your communication and interpersonal skills.
- Magnifying your creativity. By becoming more in touch with your thoughts and emotions, you can tap into the rich well within yourself that allows you to be more creative.

The foundation of breathwork is that most people have pent-up negative emotions from trauma and other painful experiences that they have suppressed. Most people leave these traumas and painful experiences unresolved, and this can cause many problems in their lives, including destructive behaviors and full-blown disorders. Breathwork encourages the revelation of the suppressed memories and emotional blocks through a state of natural induced altered state of consciousness so that we can finally be resolved these issues. This leads to the most significant benefit of breathwork, which is freedom from the past.

How to Master Your Breath in Difficult Situations

We deal with several stressful situations daily. Work, family, education, friendships, romantic relationships, driving on the interstate, just walking down the street. These and more are all situations that can have our minds racing and keep us on our tiptoes. There has been a lot of focus on the negative contribution of stress on the cardiovascular system, obesity, diabetes, high blood pressure, and mental health to name a few, but how often is the effect of stress on breathing shared?

Not enough I would assume, but a change in breathing is one of the first indications that a person needs to make a change.

One of the first things that change in your breathing when you are in a stressful situation is how you breathe. When you are breathing healthily, you breathe through your diaphragm, a muscle in the base of the chest that separates the abdomen from the chest. The diaphragm flattens and contracts when a person inhales, which causes a vacuum effect. This pulls air into the lungs. This muscle relaxes to push air out of the lungs when a person exhales.

Stress causes you to breathe through your chest instead of the diaphragm, sending a signal to your brain that you are not relaxed, and you might be in danger. This induces a fight-or-flight response and the production of the stress hormone, cortisol. This causes you to take short and erratic breaths and your muscles tense and constrict in preparation of fight or flight.

Your entire respiratory system, which allows us to breathe and includes organs such as the lungs, diaphragm and nose, goes haywire and causes your heart rate to quicken and blood pressure to spike. This compounds the negative effect on your respiratory system and causes you to breathe even faster and shallower.

This situation can escalate into a condition called hyperventilation, which is a panic response to stress, fear, or phobia. During normal breathing situations, there is a balance of inhalation and exhalation that allows the intake of oxygen and the expulsion of carbon dioxide to occur in the balance as well. During hyperventilation, this balance is disturbed because a person breathes very fast, exhaling more than they inhale. This translates into the person eliminating more carbon dioxide from the body than inhaling oxygen into the body. While carbon dioxide is a waste product of the body, it needs to be expelled in a controlled way. Low levels of carbon dioxide cause the blood vessels that supply the brain to constrict. This means that not enough blood will be supplied to the brain, and a person will experience initial symptoms like tingling of the fingers and lightheadedness. Other symptoms of hyperventilation include dizziness, shortness of breath, a lump in the throat, nausea, and confusion. If hyperventilation is not controlled and becomes severe, the person may lose consciousness.

Luckily, consciously controlling your breathing can reverse all these negative effects. The first thing you need to do is become aware of your response to stress. Next, you need to encourage breathing through your diaphragm instead of your chest. Here is a quick method to do this:

1. If possible, remove yourself from the situation that is causing you stress.
2. Sit comfortably in a quiet room and close your eyes to block out the rest of the world and concentrate internally. Tell yourself to relax and visualize that state in your mind.
3. Slowly and gently inhale air through your nose to fill your lower lungs. You will know that you have done this correctly if your stomach expands while your upper chest remains still. This is alternately called belly breathing.
4. Hold your breath for the count of three, then exhale through pursed lips. Breathe out as slowly as possible. Breathing out through pursed lips makes it easier for the lungs to function since it promotes diagrammatic breathing and improves the balance of oxygen intake and carbon dioxide outtake.

Consciously relax the muscles in your face, jaw, shoulders, stomach, and thighs.

5. Repeat steps 3 and 4 about ten more times. Concentrate on your emotions. Allow yourself to feel the negative ones such as anger and sadness, then breathe them away.

6. Open your eyes again.

If hyperventilation is occurring, modify the steps above to breathe into a paper bag or cupped hands and hold your breath for 10 to 15 seconds at a time instead.

As you calm your breath, the following things will happen:

- Your breath will slow.
- Your heart rate will go down, and your blood pressure will decrease.
- Your intake of oxygen and expulsion of carbon dioxide will once again become balanced.
- Cortisol levels in the blood will decrease.
- Muscle tension will decrease.
- Your mind calms.

Also, you can use a technique called box breathing to relieve stress and deal with difficult situations. This technique is also called four-square breathing. To do this, ensure that you are sitting upright in a comfortable chair with your feet flat on the floor in a quiet environment. Place your hands on your lap with the palms facing up and keep your spine straight. First, exhale slowly through your mouth until all the air has left your lungs. Next, inhale slowly and deeply through your nose. Count to four as you feel the air fill your lungs. Hold this breath for a count of four then exhale through your mouth again. Count to four again before you inhale. Repeat this process. The effectiveness of this technique lies in being conscious of the feeling of the air moving in and out of your lungs. It promotes the balance of oxygen intake and carbon dioxide expulsion.

Another technique for conscious breathing to handle difficult situations is called the alternate nostril breathing technique. It is a yogic breath control practice and is known as *nadi shodhana pranayama* in Sanskrit. Directly translated, it means "subtle energy clearing breathing technique." Even though it is typically done as part of a yoga and meditation practice, this conscious breathing technique can be done on its own to help calm your mind.

To practice the alternate nostril breathing technique:

1. Sit in a quiet room with your legs crossed.
2. Place your left hand on your left knee and use the thumb on your right hand to block your right nostril.
3. Inhale through your left nostril then block the left nostril with your fingers.
4. Unblock the right nostril and exhale through this side.
5. Inhale through the right nostril then use your fingers to block them.
6. Open the left nostril and exhale through the left side.
7. Repeat this process for 5 minutes and end the practice by exhaling on the left side.

In addition to helping alleviate stress, the alternate nostril breathing technique helps improve lung function, increase respiratory endurance, and improve cardiovascular function.

Finally, let's discuss the 4-7-8 breathing technique. Based on an ancient yogic technique called pranayama, it is excellent for helping people fall asleep in a shorter time. Adequate amounts of sleep help to fight stress and anxiety. As with the other breathing techniques, to begin the 4-7-8 breathing technique, you need to find a quiet, comfortable place to sit or lie down. If you are using this technique to aid in falling asleep faster, lying down is best. The first thing you need to do is rest the tip of your tongue against the roof of your mouth right behind your top front teeth. Keep your tongue in this position throughout the breathing technique. While it takes some practice to keep your tongue in place while you exhale, you will get it with time. Next:

1. Exhale through your mouth and make a whooshing sound as you let your lips fall apart.
2. Close your lips and inhale silently through your nostrils for a count of four. Hold your breath for 7 seconds.
3. Repeat Step 1. Exhale for 8 seconds.
4. Repeat the entire process for a pattern of 4 breaths.

No matter which technique you use, as you learn how to use your breath to keep calm and relaxed in difficult situations, you will find that you automatically become conscious of your breathing and avoid the negative effects that stress has on it. To compound the effects of conscious breathing, you can use practices such as meditation and mind/body exercises such as yoga and Tai Chi to promote mindfulness and a deeper awareness of the effect that breathing has on your overall being.

Chapter 2
Breathwork Practices

"When the breath is unsteady, all is unsteady; when the breath is still; all is still. Control the breath carefully. Inhalation gives strength and a controlled body; retention gives steadiness of mind and longevity; exhalation purifies body and spirit."

— Goraksasathakam

There are several ways that you can approach breathwork. My recommendation is you give them all a try to see which one resonates with you the most and continue with that one.

Shamanic Breathwork

A shaman is a healer, in the past, a shaman was thought of as a wise counselor, minister, and physician in one. This person was trusted to aid the entire community with sacred ceremonies, songs, chants, and prayers that elevated the people's spiritual beings in addition to alleviating their bodily, mental and emotional aches and pains. This breathwork technique is a process of inspiring an inner healing journey where the individual awakes and connects their inner shaman.

Traditionally, the shaman helped to restore the sacred balance of energies from the mind, body, and soul within an individual as well as encouraging healing from the inside out. They were thought to have journeyed into realms beyond the physical to achieve this with the assistance of spirit guides, power animals, and allies.

The shamanic breathwork process honors the practices of these ancient healers by focusing on awakening the healer within each individual on this planet. The process facilitates locating hidden aspects of one's self and, as such, the process is an individualized one. It taps into own innate wisdom through deep, circular breathing combined with chakra attuned music, the focusing of internal energy and the drawing of a mandala, which is a circular symbolism diagram to manifest the spiritual journey the breather underwent. This is typically performed in a group setting and usually lasts for 1 to 2 hours. Even though the session is mostly done in a group setting, they can also be achieved individually or over the phone.

The process usually begins by smudging the environment in which the technique will be performed with cedar, sweetgrass, and sage to establish this as a sacred, safe zone. Invocations, which are mantras used to invoke spiritual enlightenment, are chanted to enhance this. The facilitators will then encourage participants to lie down on a mat and to call upon the shaman within. The participants enter a dream-like state while drumming is happening in the background. This drumming enhances the connection with the sacred power that stems from within. Each session is different, but the aim is to clear all negative energy, reset with positive enlightenment, and reset old programming that could be holding the individual back. This also allows the person to gain clarity of focus, to recover the true self, to encourage spiritual growth and improve overall well-being. They will begin a journey through their psyche as they enter the dream-like state brought on by a breathing technique the facilitator introduces.

A typical breathing technique within this type of breathwork commences with a slow inhale for seven counts. Next, exhale for the same count. This measured breathing encourages the maintenance of oxygen intake and the release of carbon dioxide. Breathe through the nostrils. Close your eyes and imagine a bright white light emerging from your stomach and penetrating specific points on your body such as the shoulders, head, thighs, buttocks, etc. This will focus your intent for healing. Continue to inhale and exhale for counts of seven. Considered a type of hypnotism, the participant enters the dream-like state.

Vivation Breathwork

Vivation is also called synergistic breathing or "the skill of happiness." This transformational breathwork technique focuses on the improvement of overall well-being by the use of circular breathing without pauses between inhales and exhales. Circular breathing is the process of maintaining sounds by filling the cheeks with air when the lungs run low on air. The air in the cheeks is used to power the noise being made. Inhales are done through the nose to partially fill the lungs to maintain constant sound. The action can be described as inhaling while you exhale because you are dispelling air from the cheeks to make the sound while you pull in air through the nostrils to partially fill the lungs. In actuality, you are not exhaling because the air that leaves your mouth is coming from your cheeks, not your lungs.

There are four steps involved in circular breathing. The first is puffing up the cheeks as the lungs begin to lose air. Second, you push air from the cheeks while making a sound. You maintain this sounds as you inhale through the nose. You make the sound by creating a small hole in your lips. The third step involves bringing sufficient air in so that you can begin to exhale through the lungs once more. Lastly, the cheeks must be returned to their normal position.

This breathing technique is different from conscious breathing, which encourages an altered state of consciousness. It is commonly used by musicians that play a wind instrument such as a trumpet or saxophone.

Vivation is a physically pleasurable meditation that helps resolve trauma, relieve stress, and release negative emotions. It has roots from the ancient sciences of Indian Kriya and Tantra Yoga but also incorporates modern breathwork practices. The major difference that this breathwork technique has from others is that it is focused on inner body wisdom to place attention on the present where the individual can surrender to eternal bliss. The principle is that negative emotions create a block to feelings of pleasure. Therefore, by releasing these negative emotions, the natural flow of feelings of joy, happiness, and love can be perpetrated. Practicing vivation allows the person to feel energetic and whole because it requires complete relaxation, self-awareness, and a willingness to give into ecstasy.

The benefits of this breathwork technique are:

- It is self-contained and self-applied, meaning that a facilitator is not needed.
- It can be done anytime, anywhere.
- It increases self-love and self-confidence.
- It helps improve relationships through self-awareness and self-development.
- It allows you to enjoy the moment more.
- It helps reduce stress and anxiety.

Ultimately, this breathwork technique allows the practitioner to regard all emotions as valuable so that they can be resolved and integrated into the overall psychology of the person to promote wellbeing and happiness.

Transformational Breathwork

This breathing technique revolves around breathing to attain personal growth and spiritual transformation. It is a means to gain an altered state of consciousness to allow self-exploration and self-healing. This is facilitated by rapid, deep breathing, music that invokes images of the past, focus on body/mind connection and artistic expression in a sacred, safe space. This breathwork technique is a unique blend of body mapping, Kundalini Yoga, breath analysis, and metaphysics. This combination aims to facilitate physical and spiritual healing.

Body mapping is the process of consciously correcting one's body map to become more graceful, efficient, and coordinated while moving. The body map is your perception of how your body is represented in the outer world. If you perceive that this representation is flawed, then it will be reflected in your motions and vice versa. Therefore, transformational breathwork helps enhance the body map to transfer the way the body moves and operates.

Another important aspect of transformational breathwork is its integration of Kundalini Yoga techniques. This yoga style emphasizes meditation and activating the energy center of the body, just like this breathwork technique. This practice allows an individual to recognize their spiritual potential, to develop a fundamental awareness of themselves as a person, to refine that awareness, and expand that awareness by removing limiting thoughts and emotions.

The benefits of the breathwork technique include:

- Enhancing creativity.
- Increases energy levels.
- Increasing brain and willpower.
- Allowing the transformation of body, mind, and soul, especially since it removes blocks in energy, limiting thoughts and emotions.
- Encouraging inner guidance and self-trust.
- Calms the mind and promote emotional balance.
- Encouraging self-compassion and compassion toward others.
- Helping resolve addictions.

Transformational breathwork can be done in a group and individual settings and uses a circular breathing pattern and sound vibrations similar to vivation. People commonly report feeling a tingling sensation, joy, and transcended after a session. Please note that the session can become uncomfortable if you have a lot of pent up negative emotions. This can induce hyperventilation-like symptoms. However, the greater the pent-up energy, the greater the potential for transformation.

Holotropic Breathwork

As mentioned earlier, this breathwork technique translates into "moving toward wholeness." Therefore, the goal of practicing holotropic breathwork is to achieve wholeness of body, mind, and spirit. Through the practice of this technique, the aim is that the individual completes it and feels personally empowered and is encouraged to heal physically, mentally, spiritually, and emotionally. The people who have found the most success with this breathwork technique are those who have suffered severe trauma. Many are recommended to a holotropic breathing workshop by a therapist who feels that they would benefit from the session. Despite this, persons who have not suffered severe trauma also find enlightenment and enrichment from holotropic breathwork sessions.

Holotropic was developed by Stanislav and Christina Grof in the 1970s as an alternative to LSD, which became illegal in the late 1960s. LSD stands for lysergic acid diethylamide. This is a hallucinogenic drug that alters thoughts, feelings, and awareness of the person using it. Slang terms used for LSD also include Acid, Hippies, and Yellow Sunshine. This drug was outlawed because of the severe side effects that include distorted perception, flashbacks, depression, anxiety, and elevated blood pressure. Dr. Grof and his wife utilized this safer alternative of breathwork to put people into altered states of consciousness to help obtain mental and spiritual enlightenment.

Holotropic breathwork is a trademarked activity and so certification to become a facilitator needs to be gained through a training course. Holotropic breathwork is typically practiced in a group setting and usually lasts for 2 to 3 hours. However, individual sessions can be arranged. In a group setting people are usually arranged in pairs, with one person being the breather and the other, the sitter. The sitter ensures that the breeder is safe and supported during the breathwork session. A sitter does not interrupt the session unless the breather needs it. The certified facilitator guides the session by giving directions on when and how to increase the speed and rhythm of breathing.

The breather typically lies on a mat for the duration of a session and listens to repetitive music that encourages the breather to enter an alternate state of consciousness. This state has typically been described as having a very vivid dream. While in this state, the natural healing of the breather's psyche begins. This experience is unique to everyone and no two sessions at the same.

By the end of the session, each person can derive meaning from what happened so that they can continue on their journey of self-discovery. Discussion is encouraged so that the breather can share their re-experience with past trauma, the development of spiritual awareness or other feelings that they experienced. The breather is also encouraged to draw a mandala.

In future sessions, the sitters and breathers swap roles.

The benefits of practicing holotropic breathwork include the development of self-awareness, aiding in relaxation, and stress relief. It also helps develop compassion for one's self and others, learning to support other people and learning to trust in your ability to heal and reshape yourself. There are also some associated risks with this technique. There is the possibility that the breather may experience hyperventilation as well as the phenomena known as a healing crisis, which is an amplification of the feelings associated with a traumatic experience rather than healing. Because this breathing technique has potential to invoke such powerful physical and emotional responses, it is a good idea to speak with your healthcare provider before participating, especially if you suffer from any of the following conditions:

- Panic attacks
- Severe mental illness
- Pregnancy or breastfeeding
- Cardiovascular disease
- High blood pressure

- Seizures
- Glaucoma or retinal detachment
- Aneurysm
- Any condition that requires you to take medication.

While this technique has been proven safe for most practitioners, it is always good to err on the safe side.

Rebirthing Breathwork

This is also called conscious energy breathing. As mentioned, it was developed by Leonard Orr, who stated that he re-experienced his birth while in a bathtub. Therefore, the foundation of this breathwork technique lies on the premise that all humans carry with them the trauma of their own birth experience. The rebirthing breathwork technique aims to help people release energy that has been stored in the body due to suppressed trauma. This technique helps illuminate past trauma and the associated pent-up energy that has produced so that it can be released. Through this process, the breathwork practitioner goes through a rebirth of his or her consciousness.

Rebirth is defined as the process of being born a second time or getting a new beginning. This breathwork technique relies on unraveling the birth-death cycle to incorporate the body, mind, and soul in an altered started of consciousness that encourages healing of past trauma to allow a new beginning.

The rebirthing breathwork technique has many benefits, including:

- Reducing stress levels
- Increasing energy
- Releasing toxins from body cells

- Allowing the access of expanded states of consciousness to increase inner guidance and clarity of purpose.
- Allowing the resurfacing of old memories and past traumas so that they can be released in a safe, gentle way.
- Supporting the release of limiting thoughts and emotions left from childhood and past trauma.
- Increasing the feelings connecting one's inner self to the universe.
- Supporting the awakening of the person you truly are.
- Increases joy and pleasure in life and relationships
- Enhances personal expression and creativity.

The simple practice of this breathwork technique starts with the guidance of a facilitator called a "rebirther." The rebirther helps you skillfully maneuver through the materials that surface in your mind through the sessions. This person also validates your experience and helps you stay present in the moment and maintain mental clarity.

These sessions begin with discussing your issues with a certified specialist. This can take anywhere from 30 minutes to 1 hour. The rebirther then guides you through a conscious breathing session while you lie down on a mat in a safe, quiet area. A simple conscious breathing technique includes lying on your back and placing a heavy book on your belly. Take deep, full belly breaths with no pauses between inhales and exhales. Do this 50 times while being guided by your rhythm. With the rebirthers guidance, you will then reveal the material that surfaces in your mind. This will typically go on for up to 75 minutes. In this time, you will be in a dream-like state where you will relive memories, emotions, and body sensations which you will review and release. The power of this technique lies in the fact that you feel like an observer of your past, allowing you to re-interpret these events, feelings, and thoughts in a way that is conducive to spiritual enlightenment. This new perspective is what allows these pent-up energies to be released and purged from the being.

The people that benefit the most from this breathwork technique include:

- Those who have been through toxic relationships and would like to keep from repeating the same pattern of behavior.
- People who have panic attacks, phobias or suffer from anxiety.
- People who suffer from low self-esteem and shyness.
- People who feel trapped in a way of being.
- People who suffer from general feelings of unhappiness and dissatisfaction with their life.
- People who lack a sense of purpose in their life.
- People who feel like they are not living up to their true potential.

Rebirth can afford these people freedom from these issues.

Clarity Breathwork

The premise of this technique is founded on the rebirthing breathwork technique but differs in the fact that it is not just based on the trauma of birth. The clarity breathwork technique centers on addressing all issues or traumas that hinder the healthy flow of spiritual energy and breath. This technique focuses on forming a deeper internal connection with yourself so that you can be transformed passed your limiting thoughts, beliefs and the imprints left from the trauma of birth and the experiences you have had since then. The breathwork technique is so-called because it encourages the opening of the subconscious to allow the individual to attain a new level of self-awareness and clarity.

Clarity breathwork encompasses three areas. There are circular breathing, somatic exploration, and intuitive counseling. A facilitator can guide those in a group or with individuals. Somatic exploration involves the inquiry into our bodies through observation and study. *Soma* is the Greek word for 'of the body,' and this technique is intended to increase awareness through the senses of hearing, touch, sight, taste and smell. In a clarity breathwork session, your facilitator observes your spiritual energies such as the chakra and aura to give valuable feedback. This allows you to re-experience the trauma of our past, including your birth. The exception here is it provides an air of objectivity so you can relive them in a safe, gentle way to move toward newfound emotional intelligence.

The benefits of clarity breathwork include:

- Increased feelings of vitality and energy
- Reduced stress and anxiety.
- Increased clarity of thought
- Mental calm
- Improved concentration and focus
- Increased self-esteem and focus.
- Increased creativity and self-expression.
- Accelerated spiritual growth and the awakening of one's true self.
- Inner peace.

Chapter 3
Breathwork for Anxiety

"Anxiety does not empty tomorrow of its sorrows, but only empties today of its strength."

– Charles Spurgeon

Experiencing worrying thoughts and doubts is a normal part of living. An upcoming job interview, an unpaid bill, a date with someone new, a failed work project, health issues are all things that are part of daily living that can cause anxious thoughts. These can manifest themselves in a physical way such as sweaty palms, feelings of restlessness, and muscle tension. With all of the adverse effects worrying has on the body, mind, and heart, it is easy to say, "just stop worrying," but it's not always that easy.

What is Anxiety?

The sweaty palms, muscle tension, and feelings of uneasiness are all signs that your body is under stress and that the stress hormone has been activated. The worry that you can't seem to get rid of is called anxiety. Anxiety is your body's natural response to stress, and it makes people feel nervous or frightful. Stress and anxiety are part of everyday living. However, when the symptoms of anxiety become extreme, then this is a cause for concern. If these feelings are indeed interfering with normal physical, mental, and emotional function or last for periods longer than six months, then it is likely that the sufferer has an anxiety disorder.

Anxiety Disorders

Normal feelings of anxiety come and go, but do not prevent you from fully participating in your normal life. Anxiety disorders, on the other hand, are characterized by feelings that are intense and debilitating. These feelings stop you from doing the things you love and going to the places that you would like to go to. This can become so extreme that it prevents the sufferer from leaving their house or crossing the street out of fear.

Here is a list of common anxiety disorders and the way that they manifest themselves.

- Agoraphobia. This anxiety disorder is characterized by extreme avoidance of places and situations that might make the sufferer feel panicked, trapped, helpless, or embarrassed.
- Body focused repetitive behaviors. These are a cluster of habitual behaviors that the sufferers do in response to persistent anxiety. These behaviors can include hair pulling, lip biting, and skin picking.
- Generalized anxiety disorder. This is persistent and excessive worry about activities or events that are out of proportion to the activity or event. This can even occur for ordinary, everyday issues. This type of anxiety disorder normally occurs in conjunction with other anxiety disorders or a mental disorder such as depression.
- Health anxiety. This is a group of disorders that is characterized by the sufferer being preoccupied with one or more somatic symptoms of developing or pre-existing illness or disease.
- Panic disorder. This includes repeated episodes of unexpected anxiety and panic attacks, which are the result of intense fear.

These panic attacks and feelings of anxiety often lead to worry that they will occur again, and so the sufferer develops a cycle of avoiding the situation or activity.

- Post-traumatic stress disorder. This anxiety disorder develops as a result of a person going through or witnessing a major trauma.
- Separation anxiety. This is an anxiety disorder where a person experiences excessive fear that revolves around being separated from a specific person such as a spouse or blood relative.
- Social anxiety disorder. This is the anxiety disorder whereby sufferers feeling extremely nervous in social situations.

These are only a few of the different anxiety disorders that exist, and most require treatment from a medical practitioner if the symptoms persist and make living daily life difficult.

Causes of Anxiety

The cause of anxiety is not yet fully understood by the scientific community. However, there are common external factors that can contribute to the development of anxiety. They include:

- Financial stress
- Side effects of medication
- Stress in the form of emotional trauma like the death of a friend or family member.
- Stress-related to personal relationships like in a romantic relationship.
- The use of illicit drugs like heroin or cocaine as well as withdrawal from these drugs.
- Being a symptom of medical illness like heart attack.

It has been shown that people who are already prone to developing anxiety can be pushed into developing full-blown anxiety disorders by traumatic life experiences like abuse and the death of loved ones. There are also risk factors such as genetics, drug and alcohol abuse, personality, and childhood trauma that increase the chances of developing persistent anxiety.

Symptoms of Anxiety

Common symptoms of anxiety include:

- Increased heart rate
- Rapid breathing (hyperventilation)
- Trouble concentrating on anything other than the current cause of tension
- Feelings of weakness or fatigue
- Sweating
- Trembling
- Headaches
- Irritability
- Feelings of impending doom, panic or danger
- Trouble falling and staying asleep
- Experiencing gastrointestinal problems

Anxiety vs. Stress

Stress and anxiety are often confused because they both exhibit a lot of the same symptoms. Some of the physical symptoms that they share include rapid heart rate, muscle tension, and headaches while other symptoms may include lack of concentration, trouble sleeping, and irritability. With so many shared symptoms, it might be difficult to distinguish anxiety from stress, but this section is dedicated to eliminating that confusion.

Stress is a short-term experience in response to a trigger such as a job interview or almost getting hit by a vehicle. Stress is typically caused by an external factor, which makes it treatable by removing these factors from the sufferer's environment. Stress does not have to be negative and can be the push a person needs to perform better in a given situation. The negativity arises when stress leads to issues like insomnia and impaired ability to do the things that you usually do.

Anxiety, on the other hand, is a sudden condition that is triggered by stress. Unlike stress, which fades away when the trigger of the stress is eliminated, anxiety can persist even after. This persistence can lead to impaired social, occupation, and daily function. The origin of anxiety is internal, which makes it more difficult to treat. Because the threat is internal, it is often challenging to identify the cause, another contributing factor in the difficulty of obtaining proper treatment.

How to Release Anxiety through Breathing

As mentioned earlier, stress and therefore, anxiety-induced chest breathing, which causes the release of cortisol and puts the body in fight-or-flight mode. It upsets the balance of oxygen being taken into the body and carbon dioxide leaving the body. This imbalance contributes to the worsening of panic attacks and anxiety. By getting your breathing under control and restoring this balance, you help fight stress and reduce anxiety. Here are a few breathing techniques you can employ to beat anxiety.

Breathing through the Diaphragm

Remember that breathing through the diaphragm promotes a balance of oxygen intake and carbon dioxide expulsion as well as keeps you calm. To ensure that you work the air through your diaphragm instead of your chest, ensure that you are seated or lying in a comfortable position with your shoulders, neck and head in a relaxed position. Ensure that your knees are bent. Next, place a hand under your rib cage and the other hand over your heart. Inhale through your nose and exhale through pursed lips. Ensure that your belly moves more than your chest as you inhale and exhale. Do this for up to 10 minutes about three times a day.

Focused Breaths

Deep breathing that is slow and focused also helps reduce anxiety. Begin this by sitting or lying down in a neutral, safe environment. Breathe in and out normally, and examine how your body feels as you do this. This allows you to explore where the tension is located in your body.

Next, inhale deeply and slowly through your nose. Ensure that your belly expands more than your chest as you do this. Exhale slowly, sighing if you wish. This expels the tension that you carry. Do this for as long as you need and pay attention to the rise and fall of your belly. As you inhale, imagine that you are being washed over by waves of calmness. Imagine that any negative thoughts and energies that you carry within you are being taken away every time that you exhale. Ensure that you do not become distracted during this process for maximum effect.

The Lengthened Exhale

Deep inhales during anxiety attacks can actually increase the severity of the attack because inhales are linked to the sympathetic nervous system, controlling the fight-or-flight response. On the other hand, exhaling is associated with the parasympathetic nervous system, this helps the body relax. Too many quick breaths cause you to hyperventilate, especially in an anxious situation. Therefore, conscious lengthening of your exhales can help reduce anxiety and calm your mind.

To do this, push the air out of your lungs in counts of six while inhaling for counts of four. This makes your exhale slightly longer than your inhales. Do this for 2 to 5 minutes while seated or lying in a comfortable position in a neutral, calm environment.

Lion's Breath

This breathing exercise expands on the one outlined above by promoting exhaling forcefully. The practice gets its name from the fierce lion-like expression on the practitioner's face during exhales. The pose used and the rhythm of breathing are well-known in the yogi community to reduce anger, stress and anxiety.

To practice the lion's breath, get into a kneeling position in a safe, calm environment. Ensure that your ankles are crossed and that your behind is resting on your feet. If the kneeling position is uncomfortable for you, sit cross-legged.

As you bring your hands to your knees and stretch out your arms and fingers, breathe in through your nose then out through your mouth as you vocalize a short sound. While you exhale, open your mouth as wide as you can and stick your tongue out as far down as it can go. Focus on the end of your nose or the middle of your forehead as you exhale.

Relax your face when you inhale. Repeat the entire process six times. Change the cross of your ankles halfway through the process.

Equal Breathing

This breathing technique stems from the ancient practice of pranayama yoga, and it involves inhaling for the same amount of time that you exhale. This balance helps to reduce anxiety. Begin the breathing exercise by ensuring that you are lying or sitting down in a position that you are comfortable. Do this in a safe and calm environment. Close your eyes and breathe normally. Pay attention to what is going on in your body and locate the tension. Inhale through your nose and slowly count to four. Next, exhale and do the same slow count to four. As you continue to repeat this inhale and exhale process, be mindful of the feelings in your body and the sense of fullness and emptiness in your lungs as you breathe.

Resonate Breathing

This breathing technique is also called coherent breathing. It helps induce a relaxed state and calms anxiety. To begin, lie down and close your eyes in a neutral, safe environment. With your mouth closed, breathe in gently through your nose for a count of six. Do not overfill your lungs with air. Next, exhale for six seconds. Gently allow the air to leave your body. Continue this process for up to 10 minutes. In this time, you should notice that your heart rate mimics the calm rhythm of your breathing. This breathing technique is so effective at reducing anxiety because it helps synchronize breath with heart rate, which aids in the balance of oxygen coming into the body and carbon dioxide leaving.

Alternate Nostril Breathing

This breathing technique is a great one for improving mental focus and concentration as well as reducing anxiety as it facilitates the provision of equal amounts of oxygen to the brain while expelling carbon dioxide in the same quantity. For an in-depth outline of how to perform this breathing practice, please refer to *Chapter 1: How To Master Your Breath in Difficult Situations.*

Meditation to Reduce Anxiety

In addition to employing the breathing techniques outlined above to fight anxiety, you can make use of meditation to help alleviate the symptoms.

What is Meditation?

There has been some confusion about what meditation is. Before I explain what it is, let's take a moment to discuss what it is not.

Meditation is not about making yourself evolve into a new, different, or even better person. While you practice meditation, the purpose is not to turn off your feelings or thoughts. Meditation is not a religion.

Instead, meditation is a technique that allows the mind to become inwardly focused, clear, and relaxed so that it functions more efficiently. Meditation is a continual process that helps retrain your brain to process thoughts and feelings in new ways. Meditation relies on principles and science that allow the practitioner to gain a new awareness of themselves as well as a sense of perspective. All of this is aimed at enabling them to understand himself or herself better.

This newfound awareness leads to being more mindful. Mindfulness is the ability that a person develops so that they can be present in each moment and fully engaged in whatever activity they are doing. Mindfulness teaches you to recognize harmful and self-defeating thought patterns and behaviors so that you can steer yourself onto a more constructive course.

To manage and reduce anxiety, the first thing that is needed is an understanding of what is triggering it and how it operates. Meditation allows for inward reflection and understanding. Anxiety comes from the inability to regulate your emotions internally, and meditation helps reprogram the pathways in the brain that help this regulation hence improving one's personal ability to control their emotions so an anxiety attack can be prevented. Meditation allows you to familiarize yourself with the thoughts and feelings that induce anxiety within you. By becoming familiar with these triggers, you can release yourself from their grip because you will realize that these thoughts and feelings do not define you or your reactions to them.

With the self-awareness that comes with meditation, you will also become conscious of what your body is feeling in each moment including during an anxiety attack. This allows you to become more prepared and even better able to stop anxiety before it even starts.

Benefits of Meditation

The benefits of meditation extended far and wide and supported by science. While of course, you can use meditation to help relieve stress, reduce anxiety and get peace of mind, there are many more physical, emotional and mental benefits that should encourage you to continue practicing meditation. These benefits include:

- Reduced risk of developing cardiovascular diseases. Since there is a reduction in stress levels when you practice meditation, stress hormones are not released into the bloodstream, so heart rate and blood pressure remain balanced. This balance keeps your heart healthy and in good working order which lowers the risk of developing cardiovascular diseases such as heart attack and stroke.

- Increased energy levels. A significant part of proper meditation is controlling your breath. This ensures that oxygen and carbon dioxide levels remain balanced in the body, which allows it to stay calm and relaxed. With a proper balance of oxygen and carbon dioxide in the body, red blood cells remain properly oxygenated, leading to higher levels of energy.

- Better immunity. Decreased levels of stress and anxiety mean that the body is better able to fight off diseases. The body often inadvertently attacks itself under stressful and anxious conditions. With lowered stress and anxiety levels, the body can better regulate its immune responses.

- Better sleep. Reduced stress and anxiety levels allow the body to fall into a restful state easier, resulting in better quality and adequate quantity of sleep.

- Better emotional health. A side effect of stress and anxiety is decreased self-image and a negative outlook on life, which can lead to depression. The hormones that are released during stress and anxiety can also negatively affect the sufferer's mood. Meditation allows the practitioner to become aware of these emotions and therefore, to better control them so that they can gain a more positive and happier outlook on life.

More benefits of meditation include lengthened attention span, increased memory, concentration, focus, increased self-compassion and kindness toward others, aiding in fighting addictions as well as pain relief.

A Simple Mindful Meditation Exercise

While a meditation exercise can go on for hours, all that is needed, especially for a beginner, is a commitment of 5 to 30 minutes each day. Most people find that just 15 minutes every day is ideal. Try to do this at the same time in the same location every day so that you build a habit. Eventually, you will not have to think about doing it. Your body will go through the motions automatically.

There are several types of meditation. They include:

- Mindful meditation
- Moving meditation
- Mantra meditation
- Body scanning meditation
- Visualization meditation
- Gazing meditation

There are other types as well. Each type of meditation has its benefits, but we will focus on mindful meditation in this section. Mindful meditation involves using the breath to focus the attention of the meditation practitioner. This type of meditation relies on keeping your mind focused on the present. Your mind should not wander to the past or what you have going on in the next few minutes. You need to be still, relaxed and allow your brain and heart to heal internally. This means that you need to keep your mind from wandering or being distracted. You can keep your eyes closed to help with this, but it is not necessary if you are more comfortable with them open. If you would prefer to close your eyes but find it hard to do, try an eye mask.

If you are a newbie, staying focused will be hard to accomplish. Do not fret! When you notice your mind is starting to wander, simply refocus on your breath and bring yourself back to the present moment.

For mindful meditation to be most effective, do it in a distraction-free zone with ample time. This will let you concentrate on clearing your mind and following the rhythm of your breath. This can be anytime that is convenient for you. That may be early in the more, late at night or even on your lunch hour.

Before you start, get comfortable. Put on loose, soft clothing and unwind in your favorite way. Doing a few light stretches while listening to tranquil, soothing music can help you achieve this relaxed mindset.

Try this simple mindful meditation you can do in the comfort of your own home at any time.

1. Sit or lie down in a comfortable position. There is no set rule about what position you should take, only that you can stay in that position for some time and remain comfortable. If you choose to sit, ensure that you are not slouching and your spine is straight. Remain relaxed and put your hands on your lap. If you sit on the floor, the recommended position is cross-legged. If you sit in a chair, ensure that your feet are resting on the floor.

2. Breathe in and out slowly. Start by taking a few slow and deep breaths while you inhale through your nose and exhale through your mouth. The first few breaths are likely to be shallow but as you continue, ensure that you fill your lungs each time so that your breaths become deeper. This will make you feel calmer and more relaxed. Do not force the breathing process because this will make you tense up and defy the purpose of this practice. As you breathe, pay attention to the movement of your body such as how your belly moves, how your shoulders move up and down, how the air feels passing through your nose, etc. Pay attention to how you feel and the musings of your mind. Keep present in the moment and if your mind wanders, bring it back to the breath.

3. Open your eyes after 15 minutes have passed and move from your position.

That is it! This simple, 3-step procedure can help you reduce anxiety and many other benefits.

Guided meditation is also effective at reducing anxiety because it interrupts the pattern of thinking that facilitates stress and therefore, anxiety. Guided meditation is led by a third party which can be a yoga instructor, an audio recording or even yourself giving instructions. The third-party leads you with instructions on how to relax specific muscles in your body and with visualizations so that you get the most benefit from the meditation exercise. The added benefit of guided meditation is that someone else is there to keep you focused so that your mind does not wander. Guided meditation also offers direction and gives you a voice you can focus on during the exercise.

A Short message from the Author:

Hey, are you enjoying the book? I'd love to hear your thoughts!

Many readers do not know how hard reviews are to come by, and how much they help an author.

I would be incredibly grateful if you could take just 60 seconds to write a brief review on Amazon, even if it's just a few sentences!

>> Click here to leave a quick review

https://www.amazon.com/review/create-review?asin=B087V78F63

Thank you for taking the time to share your thoughts!

Your review will genuinely make a difference for me and help gain exposure for my work.

Chapter 4
Breathwork for Anger Management

"Every day we have plenty of opportunities to get angry, stressed or offended. But what you're doing when you indulge these negative emotions is giving something outside yourself power over your happiness. You can choose to not let little things upset you."

— *Joel Osteen*

What is Anger?

Everyone feels anger but how we deal with it is what defines us.

Anger is a powerful emotion that results from feeling hurt, frustrated, disappointed, or annoyed. Anger can vary in intensity from mild irritation to intense rage and fury. Both internal and external triggers can cause irritation. External triggers can be someone cutting you off in traffic or your boss, giving you another task at the end of an already long workday. Internal triggers might be memories of traumatic or enraging events.

Signs of anger can include:

- Grinding the teeth or clenching the jaw
- Sweating
- Trembling or shaking
- Increased and rapid heart rate
- Rapid, shallow breathing

- Increased blood pressure
- Muscle tension
- Stomach ache
- Headache
- Dizziness
- Feeling warm around the face and neck
- Feeling emotions such as sadness, guilt, resentment, and irritation
- Feeling overwhelmed
- Feeling anxious
- Feeling the need to strike out in a physical or verbal way
- Feeling like you need to get away from the situation

In extreme cases, signs of anger may include acting in an abrasive or abusive manner, yelling, screaming, crying or craving a substance to help relax.

Myths about Anger

Anger itself is not a bad thing. It is an entirely reasonable human emotion. That might surprise you to read, but there are many other misconceptions about anger circulating out there, including this one. Let's take a moment to help clear up the confusion by looking at these myths about anger.

Myth #1 - Anger is a negative emotion.

Anger is not a negative emotion, and it is very healthy that you feel it now and then. Feelings of anger can lead to positive change because it is only through feeling anger that we get up and do something. Was an injustice done to someone in your community, and you felt the need to do something about it? If your answer is yes, then a positive outcome can stem from your anger. Many laws have been passed because a large enough group felt angry about an injustice and did something about it.

Myth #2 - Anger is all in your head.

That is incorrect because you feel anger physically, emotionally, and mentally. Your face gets flushed, your body shakes, your heart rate picks up, you feel the urge to hit something, you feel betrayed. These are signs that have to do with more than just your mental process, and are all the result of anger.

Myth #3 - Anger and aggression are the same things.

They certainly are not. While anger can lead to positive change, merely reacting does not bode well for anyone. Aggressive behavior is unhealthy and can damage others, including the person who is angry in physical, emotional, and mental ways. While anger can be felt involuntarily, acting out is a choice.

Myth #4 - Ignoring anger makes it go away.

Smiling to cover up your anger or denying your feelings is called suppression and suppression of anger is unhealthy as it disturbs your peace of mind and can make you direct that anger inward. Suppressed anger has been linked to several physical and mental health problems, such as depression and hypertension. Also, suppressed anger can erupt and manifest as aggressive and abusive behavior. Finding a healthy outlet and calmly expressing your anger works a lot better.

Myth #5 - Men get angrier than women.

This is false. Men and women have the same propensity to feel anger. The difference lies in that men are more likely to show aggressive and compulsive expressions to the anger compared to women.

Myth #6 - Anger management classes and therapy do not work.

This is false. Most of the time, there are negative consequences in response to anger; it is because people do not know how to handle their emotions well. Anger management classes and therapy offer persons with anger issues, especially those who have aggressive outbursts, tools, and techniques that can help them better manage their emotions and thus, their response to anger.

Anger can be a force for positive change, or it can have a negative outcome. It all depends on how the person chooses to handle it and react to it.

Anger Disorders

Anger disorders are a pattern of behavior that includes pathological aggression and violent behaviors that are a symptom of and driven by an underlying and chronically repressed anger or rage. Most people who exhibit signs of an anger disorder have a history of mismanagement of anger, including anger suppression. This mismanagement often leads to resentment, bitterness, hatred, and rage. Anger disorders are often a symptom of other disorders like OCD and ADHD, both of which will be discussed in the next section. Substance abuse can also lead to anger disorders.

The most commonly known anger disorder is called Intermittent Explosive Disorder (IED). Sudden episodes of unwarranted anger characterize this disorder. People who suffer from this disorder describe it as losing control of their emotions and being overcome by anger. This loss of control impairs their judgment, and they may threaten or attack people, animals and objects. This disorder is normally diagnosed after a person has displayed at least three episodes of aggressive outbursts that show a lack of apparent provocation or reason.

There are a variety of factors that may lead to IED. They include genetics. While no specific gene has been located to be associated with the disorder, there has been a trend shown in families. There has also been research that indicates abnormalities in areas of the brain regulate inhibition. This abnormality can lead to impulsive violent behavior.

Environment also plays in the development of this anger disorder. Children who grow up exposed to a person with IED or who have been subjected to harsh treatment at the hands of someone in authority are likely to develop IED at an early age.

Other factors that can lead to developing IED include:

- Experiencing emotional trauma
- Experiencing physical trauma
- Some medical conditions
- A history of substance abuse
- Being male

In addition to the normal signs of anger, a person with IED can also exhibit these other symptoms:

- Physical and verbal aggression
- Damaging property
- Road rage
- Angry outbursts

- Physically attacking people, animals, and objects
- Low frustration tolerance
- Brief periods of emotional detachment

The effects of IED are far-reaching and do not only affect the sufferer. The effects that IED can have include:

- Legal issues
- Imprisonment
- Drug and alcohol abuse and addiction
- Impaired interpersonal relationships
- Trouble concentrating and focusing at home, work and school
- Low self-esteem and self-confidence
- Domestic and child abuse
- Self-harm
- Suicidal thoughts and behaviors

If you or someone you know suffers from an anger disorder, I urge you to seek help from a medical practitioner such as a therapist so that you can get the assistance you need before you do irreversible damage to yourself or others.

Causes of Anger Disorders

Anger can have several causes. These include:

- Depression. Along with the other symptoms that occur over an extended period of at least two weeks, sadness and loss of interest are often felt along with anger in this condition. This anger may be outwardly expressed and visible to others, but other times it is suppressed.

- Grief. Grief is defined as deep sorrow. There are several stages to the process of grief which can come as a result of a breakup, losing a job, the death of a loved one and more. Including anger, there are five stages of grief. The other four stages are denial, bargaining, depression, and acceptance. The anger that the grieving person will feel may be directed inward or outward.

- Alcohol abuse. Alcohol abuse, also known as alcoholism, refers to the consumption of too much alcohol at one time as well as regular use. It impairs the drinker's ability to think coherently and to make rational decisions. It has also been shown that drinking alcohol increases instances of aggression, which is a symptom of anger.

- Drug abuse. Just as with alcohol abuse, one of the consequences of drug abuse, such as heroin and cocaine abuse, is aggressive behavior which is a sign of anger.

- Traumatic experiences. Traumatic experiences, such as abuse and childhood trauma, often trigger anger and violent outbursts due to uncontrollable emotions. Anger is a coping mechanism to help this person deal with the negativity they experienced, but this anger is self-destructive. People who get angry for this reason often need the assistance of a medical practitioner such as a therapist to work through this.

- Obsessive-Compulsive Disorder. Also referred to as OCD, Obsessive-Compulsive Disorder is an anxiety disorder that is characterized by compulsive behavior and obsessive thoughts. OCD is characterized by disturbing thoughts, urges, and images that make a person do something repetitively. Anger is often a symptom of OCD because the person becomes frustrated with the inability to prevent the obsessive thoughts and behaviors.

- Attention Deficit Hyperactivity Disorder. Also known as ADHD, this is a neurodevelopmental disorder that includes symptoms such as impulsivity, hyperactivity, and inattention. These symptoms are often exhibited in early childhood and continue throughout a person's life. Anger is a symptom of ADHD.
- Bipolar disorder. This is a disorder that causes dramatic and intense shifts in mood. Anger is one of the intense emotions that a person who has bipolar disorder will feel.
- Oppositional Defiant Disorder. Sometimes referred to as ODD, this is a disorder that results in defiant and angry behavior toward authority. While this disorder is most common in children, it is also seen in adults.

What is Anger Management?

The natural way to express anger, which was passed down from early caveman, is with aggression. Anger is an adaptive response that helps human beings eliminate threats to themselves. It invokes feelings of power as well, which is why it can become addictive. In essence, anger was necessary for survival.

However, we have come a long way from our ancestors and do not need to lash out aggressively to assert dominance or state our position in a situation. We have evolved and learned to express our feelings calmly throughout the history of civilization.

It can still be difficult to suppress our instincts. As seen from the number of disorders that exhibit anger as a symptom, anger is not something that a person can always control or avoid. You can, however, learn to control your reaction. The first step in effectively managing your anger is learning to recognize the signs when you are angry. These have been listed above. You should familiarize yourself with them so that you know what to look out for. Next, you can employ strategies to manage your anger in a safe, effective way

Anger management is the process of learning to recognize that you are angry then taking proactive measures to calm down and deal with the situation that is productively angering you. There are classes and therapy available if you need help to diffuse anger. If you suffer from issues like ADHD and depression, there are also medications that your medical practitioner can prescribe to help you if needed. However, there are simple strategies that you can employ alone or in addition to the advice you receive from your doctor, in class or therapy and the effects of any medication.

You can find some of these strategies to help defuse your anger below.

Visualize yourself being calm

Calming your anger starts in your mind. Manifest a calmer, more relaxed state by imagining that you are in that state. It helps to remove yourself temporarily from the situation that is making you angry. Find a quiet place to sit, close your eyes and let your imagination show you a calm and happy version of yourself. Include the small details in your mental imagery such as what it feels like, what your facial expressions look like and even what you smell in that moment.

Remove yourself from the situation

Take a timeout. If a situation is increasing your anger level, remove yourself from it so that you can calm down and think clearly. Then, you can figure out how to handle the situation in a more productive way.

Count to 10

If you cannot remove yourself from the angering situation, you can still calm yourself down. Close your eyes if you must and slowly count to 10. As you could imagine a wave of calm washing over you. This will afford you at least 10 seconds to control your emotions and therefore, your behavior.

Think before you speak

We are often tempted to lash out when we are angry. This includes verbally. In this time, we tend to say things we do not mean or did not mean to say at that time. To avoid this verbal vomit, take a few moments to detach yourself from the situation and hold your tongue until you have calmed down.

Progressive muscle relaxation

Muscle tension is a sign of anger. By encouraging your muscles to relax, you can diffuse your anger. One method of encouraging muscle relaxation is called progressive muscle relaxation. This is often applied to different parts of the body one area at a time. For example, a relaxation technique you can apply to your abdomen is gently tightening the muscles of your stomach as you inhale. Keep from straining your muscles. As you do this, you will notice the tension. Release the tense as you exhale and pay attention to the way your muscles relax in response. Repeat this for 2 minutes. As you pay attention to the tensed and relaxed states of your muscles, you can work to bring them to a permanently relaxed state. You can then move onto another body area such as the chest and shoulders and repeat the same technique.

Exercise

Exercise and physical activities like dancing, help reduce stress, tension, and anxiety by activating the release of feel-good hormones and promoting deep breathing. This helps maintain the oxygen intake, carbon dioxide release balance. These conditions also help reduce anger as well as help you improve your mood. It is great to make this a habit but developing a schedule such as working out three mornings a week. When an action becomes a habit, it will not feel like such a chore to do. Developing a habit for exercise and physical activity is especially important if you are a person who does not like to do.

Get a support system

Try to maintain relationships with people that you can have meaningful conversations with. In that way, you can talk about your feelings and these people will help you see things from a different point of view. Understanding from another point of view can help reduce your anger. This also helps keep you from feeling isolated. Having a support system lightens the emotional load, which makes it more bearable and therefore, easier to control.

Keep a journal

In addition to talking out your feelings so that you can gain a different point of view and find closure to help reduce your anger, you can write them down. You can keep a journal, which can be a simple notebook.

By writing your thoughts and feelings down, you can examine them closer and revisit them when you are more level headed so that you can better understand what triggers your anger. This might be the turning point that allows you better control over your emotions.

Try to find humor in the situation

Laughter usually makes things better, and that list includes anger. Try to find something to laugh about in the heat of the moment. Laughter and smiling (even forced laughter and fake smiles) release more of those feel-good hormones, which elevates the mood and reduces anger.

Practice listening

Anger often arises because of miscommunication between people. Communication is the process of one party, sending a message to be interpreted by another party. Communication is only effective if the latter party receives and understands the message as it was intended. Active listening is part of proper communication. Improving your listening skills can help you communicate better. You may find that you are no longer so easy to anger because of this.

Control the way you breath

One of the most effective natural methods of controlling anger is by learning to breathe your way through it. This is explained more in-depth below.

How to Cope With Anger through Breathing

As you might have noted, one of the symptoms of anger is rapid, shallow breathing. This forces you to breathe through your chest rather than your diaphragm. This has all the usually internal reactions such as an imbalance of oxygen intake and carbon dioxide release and the release of stress hormones. One of the ways to control your anger is by slowing and deepening your breath.

To ensure that whatever breathing exercise that you practice is effective, try to find a quiet, comfortable place. This can be in your bed, in your car or even while you sit on the toilet. The location does not matter. What matters is that you have a distraction-free neutral and comforting place to practice. You also need to ensure that you are relaxed and your muscles are at ease. Use the progressive muscle relaxation technique to release any tenseness. Pay attention to your facial features as well, and notice the way they react when you inhale and exhale.

While you can, of course, try breathing exercises in the heat of the moment to calm your anger and feelings of rage, you can also practice breathing for anger daily so you become more mindful and self-aware. This allows you to control yourself better when you are angry rather than having to deal with the fallout of a negative reaction.

Some of the breathing techniques that we have already discussed in previous chapters also help with reducing anger. They include:

- Lion's breath
- Focused breaths
- Breathing through the diaphragm
- 4-7-8 breathing technique

Also, here are a few more breathing techniques that can help you overcome the intensity of your anger. Some of these include yoga poses that are highly concentrated on breathwork.

Complete Breath

This breathing technique concentrates on imagery as it allows you to picture the negativity that builds as a result of anger leaving your body with every exhale. To do it, sit cross-legged with your spine straight. Inhaling deeply and slowly, bringing your breath into your diaphragm. Place your hand over your chest and allow your ribcage to rise with this inhale. Hold this pose for three counts then exhale completely and imagine that your negative thoughts and emotions leave your body with the air. Repeat until you feel purged those negative thoughts and emotions.

Breathing for Relaxation

As the title suggests, this breathing technique is used for getting into a state of relaxation. It can also be used to blow away anger, stress, and anxiety. For relaxation, lie on your back in a comfortable position and allow your body to drain of all tension. Place your right hand on your chest and your left hand over your abdomen. Breathe deeply and let your natural rhythm take over. Your inhales and exhales should equate to the same amount of time. As you inhale and exhale, allow only your left-hand rise and fall. Your right hand should remain motionless.

Corpse Pose

This yoga pose is great for calming the body and mind as well as allowing the practitioner to focus on the natural rhythmic state of them breathing, which aids in relaxation. To do this pose, lie on your back with your arms relaxed at your sides. Your palms should be facing up. Allow your feet to fall open comfortably. Breathe in and out through your nose and allow the air to pass through your diaphragm. Let the natural rhythm of your breathing take over and concentrate on the sound of air entering and leaving your body until you feel completely relaxed. Do not allow your mind to wander, and if it does bring it back to the present moment and re-concentrate on the sound of your breathing.

Child's Pose

This yoga pose is said to be wonderful for strengthening the connection between the mind and body and for keeping you in touch with how you feel. This is great for allowing you to handle your anger in a productive and come manner. To get into this pose, kneel on all fours on a comfortable mat. Bring your arms around to the sides of your body as you push back and allow your head to rest on the floor. Reach your arms out in front of you to extend your shoulders for an extended child's pose.

Other Forms of Meditation for Anger

Consistently and repeatedly practicing meditation allows the practitioner to better control and cope with their negative emotions such as anger. This management and control allow them to react to the anger in a way that they wish rather than just going with the ebb and flow of the emotion. By practicing meditation, you learn to respond to anger rather than react to it. There is a science to how this works, and here it is. Meditation encourages the practitioner to enter a mindful and self-aware state. This instantly calms the person and lowers their stress levels. This has the effect of lowering the production of cortisol. This magnifies the calm of the mind and increases focus and clarity. When your mind is calm, you are less likely to become angry. In this way, you learn to make rational decisions even in situations that would have otherwise angered you and triggered you to react without thought.

Meditation is a practice that relies on breathing techniques, and as such, it allows sufficient oxygen to enter the blood and travel to the brain for optimal performance. Meditation also promotes elevated moods, which increases the production of feel-good hormones in the body. When you feel happy, you are less likely to become angry.

Meditation also allows you to rewire the way that you think and behave during certain situations, even in times of anger. We all develop habits in response to certain situations and emotions, including anger. Some of these habits in response to anger may be lashing out verbally. Meditation allows you to think more clearly and to effectively let go of these bad habits so that you do not act out in an undesirable manner. Since meditation will enable you to balance your emotions better and to think more rationally, you can review the situation that may have provoked your anger from a different perspective and see a way out of it that is easy for everyone involved. Meditation really can be a game-changer in allowing you to react to anger in a productive, safe, and friendly way.

Here is a simple, 20-minute meditation exercise you can practice daily to help you calm your emotions and your mind for better anger management.

1. In a quiet comfortable room, sit in a cross-legged position.
2. Gently rest your hands on your thighs with your palms up. Pull your shoulders back and pay attention to the sensations in your body.
3. You have the choice of keeping your eyes open or closing them. If you choose to keep your eyes open, try not to become distracted during this 20-minute session.

4. Focus inward on your navel. Begin to breathe slowly and deeply through your diaphragm. Every time you inhale or exhale count from one to ten, then back down to one. Every time you inhale, hold on to the tension at that location at your navel. Every time that you exhale release that tension with your breath

5. Repeat this five times.

6. Now, it is time to visualize an incident that triggered your anger. Allow yourself to picture the details and acknowledge your anger by saying, "I am angry." Repeat the statement ten times. Vary the pitch of your voice every time that you say it, such as in a louder, softer, faster, and then slower tone.

7. Allow yourself to check for any other emotions that you felt during the incident that angered you. Once you have identified the emotion, again say this out loud in varying pitches. For example, you may say, "I feel embarrassed."

8. Concentrate on your breath once more and every time that you exhale, imagine that you exhale that negative emotion. Resume counting from 1 to 10 and back down to one until the 20-minute period is over.

9. Allow yourself to stay present and do not concentrate on any particular thought once you have settled the angering issue in your mind. If your thoughts start to interrupt your counting, refocus on your breath, and count again from one.

The exercise is as simple as that, but after those 20 minutes, you should feel a lot calmer and more relaxed, especially if you had experienced anger directly before this. The exercise allowed you to relive the moment but to then react calmly to it and to gain relaxation. This builds the muscle memory of how you should respond in the moment of anger.

Chapter 5
Breathwork for Chronic Pain

"That pain moves when you move; it mutters between every breath; it spikes your ears; it rips. You think pain can't be any more horrible than that. Until you discover that the well is bottomless. There's always more."

— Ilsa J. Bick

What is Chronic Pain?

We all know how pain feels. It is a sensation that hurts and causes discomfort and unpleasant feelings.

Despite how it may feel, pain is a good thing and an essential reaction of the nervous system to help alert you of the possibility that you have been injured. When you have been injured, pain signals travel from the injured area to the spinal cord and brain. The brain takes corrective measures to heal the injury and eventually stop the pain

Pain is a sign that something is going wrong in the body and the severity of that pain often depends on the severity of whatever is going wrong. Pain allows us to judge what this something might or might not be and how it can be fixed. Usually, when we fix the problem, the pain goes away. That is not the case with chronic pain.

Chronic pain is also known as persistent pain, pain that goes on for longer than 12 weeks despite treatment or medication. It is defined as pain that extends beyond the point that healing would be expected to be complete. This period is usually 3 to 6 months.

Chronic pain can be steady or intermittent, going and coming without any apparent reason. It can feel dull or sharp and can affect different areas in different ways.

Chronic pain can be debilitating because it can limit your mobility, reduce your flexibility, strength, endurance, and make daily tasks and activities quite challenging. Chronic pain is a serious issue that is wide-reaching. It is estimated that more than 1.5 billion people around the world suffer from this condition.

Acute Pain vs. Chronic Pain

Before we take a more in-depth look at what chronic pain is, let's take a moment to specify what makes it different from acute pain.

Acute pain is caused by something specific and usually comes on suddenly. It is short in quality and goes away when the underlying cause of the pain has been treated. Acute pain does not last longer than six months and is usually caused by the following reasons:

- Broken bones
- Burns
- Cuts
- Surgery
- Labor and childbirth

When the underlying issues that caused the acute pain have been treated, life for that person typically goes on as usual.

Chronic pain is altogether different and continues to persist even after the injury or illness that caused it has been treated and healed. The pain signals in that area remain active for weeks, months, and even years. The kicker is that chronic pain does not even need to stem from a history of injury or damage to any particular body part. Chronic can start one day with no apparent cause.

There are certain conditions that chronic pain is linked to, and they include:

- Headache and migraine. While a headache is limited to pain in and around the head, a migraine has additional symptoms like nausea and sensitivity to light.
- Cancer. An uncontrolled growth of cells that invade body tissues.
- Arthritis. This is an inflammation of the joints.
- Diabetes. A disease that occurs when blood sugar levels are too high.
- Irritable bowel syndrome, which is a chronic condition that causes inflammation in the digestive tract.
- Interstitial cystitis. This is a chronic disorder characterized by pain and pressure in the bladder.
- Nerve pain. Also called neuralgia or neuropathic path and is caused by the misfire of pain signal due to nerve injury or damage.
- Back pain. This can be caused by a variety of reasons such as vigorous activity, injury and prior medical conditions.
- Fibromyalgia, widespread pain in the muscles and bones.
- Endometriosis, which is a disorder that occurs when the uterine lining grows outside of the uterus.

- Vulvodynia. This is chronic pain in the vulva that occurs with no apparent cause.
- Chronic fatigue syndrome. This is a condition that is characterized by a prolonged and extreme weariness that is often accompanied by pain.
- Temporomandibular joint dysfunction. This condition causes painful clicking locking or popping of the jaw.
- Post-surgery.
- Post-trauma, such as blunt force trauma.

While both acute pain and chronic pain can be debilitating and can affect a person's life in many ways, chronic pain is ongoing, unlike acute pain which has a limited duration.

Types of Chronic Pain

The first type of chronic pain is called nociceptive pain, which is pain that is detected by specialized sensory moves called nociceptors. The job of nociceptors is to recognize painful stimuli and then send information to the spinal cord and brain so that the response can be made. There are two types of nociceptive pain. They are visceral pain and somatic pain.

Visceral pain refers to pain that is detected by nociceptors in internal organs. Visceral pain is often dull and hard to locate, especially since the pain can be felt for the away from the actual origin. Examples of visceral pain include bladder pain, irritable bowel syndrome, prostate pain, and endometriosis.

Somatic pain refers to pain that is detected by nociceptors in the skin, muscles, and soft tissues. Unlike visceral pain, this type of chronic pain is usually easy to locate because the sensory nerves are well-distributed in the soft tissue. The pain is usually sharper in nature compared to visceral pain. Examples of somatic pain include arthritis, headaches, and back pain.

The next type of chronic pain is neuropathic pain. This is caused by nerve disturbances and automatic transmission of pain signals to the brain by malfunctioning nerves. This type of chronic pain is often described as shooting or sharp. Possible reasons for the development of neuropathic pain include nerve damage, nerve irritation, and neuroma formation. A neuroma is a benign (non-cancerous) growth of nerve tissue between the third and fourth toes. Referred to as a nerve tumor or a pinched nerve, it causes pain, tingling, burning sensation, and numbness. Examples of neuropathic pain include post-mastectomy pain, phantom limb pain, and sciatica, which is back pain caused by a problem with the sciatic nerve. The sciatic nerve is a large nerve that runs from the lower back to the back of each leg.

Psychogenic pain is the next type of chronic pain that we will discuss. This type of pain is caused by psychological disorders such as anxiety and depression. These psychological disorders manifest themselves in physical symptoms such as fatigue and pain. Due to the nature of the origin of this pain, it is difficult to treat.

Lastly, idiopathic pain is chronic pain that manifests with no known physical or psychological cause. This type of chronic pain is common in people with pre-existing pain disorders such as fibromyalgia.

Causes of Chronic Pain

Chronic pain is typically initiated by an injury such as a pulled muscle. The science community believes that chronic pain often develops after the nerves in the affected area become damaged. Damaged nerves make the pain more intense and longer-lasting. Unfortunately, treating the underlined injury does not make chronic pain go away.

As mentioned before, injury is not the only way that chronic pain develops. Sometimes there is no prior injury, and the exact cause of chronic pain in that instance is not well understood by the science community. Chronic pain may arise from underlying health conditions such as fibromyalgia, chronic fatigue syndrome, and irritable bowel syndrome.

Certain risk factors increase your chance of developing chronic pain. These risk factors include:

- Advancing in age
- Being overweight or obese
- Being female
- Being injured
- Having surgery
- Sleep disturbances
- Alcohol and drug abuse
- Smoking

How to Cope With Pain by Just Breathing

Luckily people who suffer from chronic pain do not have to deal with its debilitating consequences forever there are treatment options. These options include:

- Medication. This includes over the counter pain relievers like acetaminophen (Tylenol) and aspirin (Advil), and opioid pain relievers which includes morphine.

- Medical procedures. This list is quite extensive and includes nerve block, which is a procedure that prevents nerves from sending pain signals to the brain. Acupuncture which involves lightly pricking the skin with needles to alleviate pain. Electrical stimulation, which helps reduce chronic pain by sending mild electric shocks into the muscles. The option of surgery is also available to correct injuries that have healed improperly and may be contributing to chronic pain.
- Pain management programs. These are psychologically-based rehabilitative, group-based programs designed for people with persistent pain. These are guided by experienced health care professionals.
- Alternative medicine. This is not very well supported, but some people have reported success with a technique like hypnosis and medical marijuana.
- Lifestyle changes. Some people have found relief by adding activities that help manage the pain to their normal routine. This can include trying yoga, music and art therapy, getting massages and participating in physical therapy.

Using breathing techniques can also help with dealing with chronic pain in a natural, safe, and effective way. Chronic pain has several physical and emotional effects on the body and mind. The physical effects include the tensing of muscles, lack of energy and appetite changes while emotional effects include depression, anger, fear, and anxiety. This can make daily living very difficult, indeed. However, with a concerted effort at relaxing and deep breathing, chronic pain sufferers can make the symptoms more bearable. Learning to relax while in pain can be difficult, but it is certainly possible. Here is a breathing technique that can help you relax and therefore lower your pain levels.

Go to a dark room and place yourself in a reclined and relaxed position. Keep your eyes shut or focused on a particular point that is close to you. Breathe in and out deeply through your diaphragm and allow your mind to stay focused while you repeat the word relax in your head. You can say the word out loud by saying "re" as you inhale and "lax" as you exhale. As you allowed this slow control and deep breathing to soothe you, enhance the relaxing effect by using imagery techniques. These techniques are also involved in meditation, so they are outlined in the following section.

Other Meditation for Chronic Pain

Pain can be a stressful thing to deal with. As a result, all of the associated consequences of dealing with stress are involved in dealing with pain. As we have discussed earlier, meditation is a great activity for reducing stress levels and can help you better cope with the pain of chronic pain. Common meditative practices that are used to deal with pain relief include mindful meditation, yoga, Tai Chi, and meditation with guided imagery. Meditation with guided imagery begins by practicing and deep breathing techniques such as the one outlined in the section above. This breathing technique can be combined with soothing music. Imagery techniques include:

- Sensory splitting, which is a technique that divides sensations such as pain and burning. Therefore, if you feel a painful burning sensation on your arm, focus on one of these sensations while ignoring the other.

- Altered focus. This is a technique that allows the mind to alter the sensation that the body experiences. In practice, the person will focus their attention on the part of the body that is not in pain and alter the sensation in the body parts so that they could focus away from the area that is in pain. For example, to take your mind off the pain in your arm, you may imagine a tingling sensation in your knee.

- Disassociation. This imagery technique involves mentally separating the parts of the body that are in pain away from the rest. The chronic pain sufferer can also imagine that the mind and body are separate so that they can distance their mind from physical pain.

- Positive imagery, the practice of mentally focusing attention on a pleasant place or experience, like traveling to a foreign country, rather than focusing on the pain.

- Pain movement. With this technique, the person mentally moves the pain from one body part to another, where it is more bearable.

- Counting. This is a technique that distracts the sufferer as the person may count objects such as tiles or mental images. This is an effective technique for a distraction from the pain.

- Mental anesthesia. This technique involves imagining that numbing anesthetic has been injected into the painful area. This mental imagery allows the brain to trick the body into believing that the pain has indeed been treated.

- Mental analgesia. This technique works similarly to the one described above and only differs in that the projected image is one of a strong painkiller being administered.

- Transfer. This involves the movement of a pleasant, altered sensation to the painful area. For example, you can imagine the sensation of a feather lightly touching your skin instead of the painful sensation being experienced.
- Symbolic imagery. This technique allows you to imagine that the pain is something that annoys you like a loud noise. You then mentally give yourself the power to slowly turn that loud noise down is that your pain is also reduced in the process.

These are only a few of the imagery techniques that you can use while practicing deep breathing. These imagery techniques can only be effective if the practitioner continues to take these deep and soothing breaths and keeps their mind concentrated on the present moment.

Another great meditative practice is called walking meditation. This involves walking as the name suggests. The practitioner concentrates on the movement of their legs and feet and on the sensation of taking steps. This simple act of concentration takes the mind off any lingering pain.

Chapter 6
Breathwork for Trauma

"Even in times of trauma, we try to maintain a sense of normality until we no longer can. That, my friends, is called surviving. Not healing. We never become whole again ... we are survivors. If you are here today... you are a survivor. But those of us who have made it thru hell and are still standing? We bare a different name: warriors."

— *Lori Goodwin*

What is PTSD?

PTSD stands for Post-Traumatic Stress Disorder. This is a psychiatric disorder that occurs in people who have witnessed or experienced a traumatic event such as violent personal assault, acts of war, combat or a natural disaster. PTSD went by other names in the past such as shell shock during World War I, and combat fatigue after World War II. As a result, it is commonly associated with soldiers or older persons who have been through war such as veterans. But the fact is that PTSD does not only affect people who have been through warlike situations.

Anyone who has been through a type of traumatic experience can suffer the same symptoms of post-traumatic stress disorder. This psychiatric disorder is characterized by disturbing and intense thoughts and feelings that are related to the traumatic experience even long after the traumatic event has ended. These people often relive the traumatic event or experience through nightmares and flashbacks that cause extreme negative emotions like sadness, anger, and fear. This can also put a hole in the person's self-esteem, self-confidence, and their perceived self-worth.

As a result of this extreme emotional effect, persons with PTSD are often estranged from other people or feel detached from society since they typically like to avoid people and situations that could remind them of the traumatic event. Even if the person was not directly involved in the event or situation, PTSD can make it very difficult to resume a normal life. Something as simple as an unexpected noise or an accidental touch can trigger a flashback and the unsettling consequences that come with it. The symptoms of PTSD can be debilitating and interfere with the day-to-day functioning of the person who suffers from it. Therefore, getting effective treatment for PTSD symptoms is vital to resume normal function.

Symptoms of PTSD

PTSD symptoms often start soon after the traumatic event, such as within one month, but it is not unheard of for them to appear even years after the event.

PTSD does not just take a mental and emotional toll on the person suffering. There are physical ramifications, as well.

The symptoms of PTSD are placed in these four categories:

Avoidance Symptoms

This is characterized by the person who suffers from PTSD avoiding situations, people, and places that might trigger bad memories of their traumatic experience. Part of this avoidant technique may involve not speaking or thinking about the event at all. While the PTSD suffer might try to find relief from the troubling thoughts, feelings, and memories with avoidance, this is of no help since it prevents that person from confronting the event and therefore, moving past it to living a healthier, happier life. No matter how much this person tries to avoid the traumatic experience or reminders of it, it eventual resurfaces in their behavior patterns, thoughts, dreams, and more.

Intrusive Thoughts

This includes involuntary and repeated memories, flashbacks and distressing dreams that are centered around a traumatic event. Flashbacks can be severe and so vivid that a person feels like they are reliving the traumatic event and seen it before their very eyes. For example, if a person with PTSD is an army veteran and has a flashback to a shootout during wartime, he or she might not see or hear the crowd anymore. Instead, this person may become immersed in the events unfolding in their mind and react to the past memory rather than what is actually going on. Nightmares can even make this person reenact the traumatic events with actions such as sleepwalking and screaming while in the throws of a dream. This can also cause physical symptoms such as sweating and increased and rapid heartbeat.

Cognitive Symptoms

These symptoms include negative thoughts directed inward and outward. They affect how the person thinks and feels. As a result, this person may take to bashing themselves and their character. The effects also include feeling hopeless about the future, having memory problems like not remembering specific parts of the traumatic event, feeling guilt or shame over the event. It can also illicit the person to feel detached from friends, family and local community, or have difficulty maintaining close relationships. The activities or hobbies they once enjoyed leave them feeling emotionally numb and they will also experience difficulty in staying positive. Due to a negative mental environment, the person with PTSD is likely to develop a mental disorder such as depression and persistent anxiety. This person is also likely to shut themselves away socially, which makes PTSD and these other disorders all the harder to treat.

Hyperarousal Symptoms

This involves a high level of reactivity from the person living with PTSD. This includes changes in the physical and emotional reactions this person has. The changes are usually a stark difference compared to their reactions before they suffered the traumatic incident. These changes may include always being on guard, feeling in danger, trouble concentrating, trouble sleeping, feeling overwhelming often, feeling degrees of shame and guilt over the incident, exhibiting aggressive behavior and angry outbursts, being easily startled or frightened and exhibiting self-destructive behaviors such as alcoholism and driving too fast. Younger children may also show symptoms such as re-enacting the traumatic event or aspects of the traumatic event while they play and having thoughts and dreams that may not include elements of the traumatic event.

The intensity and combination of symptoms vary from person to person, and even from time to time. Some people may only exhibit PTSD symptoms when they are stressed while other people may need a trigger like a loud noise or being touched without permission. The symptoms of PTSD can be very severe, indeed. If you have PTSD and you find that the symptoms are getting worse or you have self-harm or suicidal thoughts, please get help right away. You can reach out to a trusted friend or colleague, contact a spiritual leader in your community, make an appointment with your doctor, mental health practitioner, or call the suicide hotline in your country.

Types of PTSD

There are five main types of PTSD. They are:

Acute Stress Disorder

The characteristics of this type of PTSD include mental confusion, disassociation, severe insomnia, being unable to assume basic self-care daily, and panicked reactions. Treatment for this includes removal from the scene of trauma, brief supportive psychotherapy, immediate support, and if needed medication to deal with anxiety insomnia and grief. This type of PTSD typically starts to exhibit symptoms within one month of the traumatic incident. The sufferer must exhibit symptoms for a minimum of 3 days to be diagnosed. The sufferer often re-experiences the traumatic event and therefore, tries to avoid reminders of that incident such as conversations, thoughts, places, and activities as much as possible. This person typically has trouble sleeping, is irritable, and has an exaggerated response.

Normal Stress Response

This occurs when a healthy adult has been exposed to a singular traumatic event in adulthood that inspires intense bad memories, feelings of unreality, distressing emotions, numbness, and cutting themselves off from relationships. A normal stress response is actually a precursor to full-blown PTSD and is typically experienced after something like an injury, accident, illness, or abandonment has occurred. Abnormal amounts of stress and tension lead to a normal stress response. Recover from this usually occurs within a few weeks when counseling is sought out. This counseling usually begins with the sufferer describing the traumatic events and the emotions that are related to events. Recovery is possible with education on how they can cope with the symptoms of PTSD.

Uncomplicated PTSD

Uncomplicated PTSD is a result of a person experiencing a singular major traumatic event rather than a series of traumatic events. This fact makes it easier to treat. This type of PTSD is characterized by persistent re-experiencing of the traumatic event, emotional numbness, symptoms of hyperarousal, and avoidance of stimuli associated with the traumatic event. A combination of approaches can be used to treat this, such as group therapy and medication.

Complex PTSD

This is sometimes called a disorder of extreme stress or complicated PTSD, and it is normally something that is experienced by persons who have been exposed to traumatic circumstances over a prolonged time, such as domestic abuse. People with this type of PTSD often also diagnosed with borderline or antisocial personality disorders. They typically exhibit behavioral problems such as aggression, eating disorders, drug and alcohol abuse, and impulsivity. This person might often experience extreme emotions such as intense rage depression and panic and have difficulties with mental functions such as disassociation, amnesia, and fragmented thoughts. Persons with this type of PTSD often take longer to respond to treatment and require a highly structured treatment program to gain results.

Comorbid PTSD

This type of PTSD is normally associated with another major psychiatric disorder such as alcohol and substance abuse, depression, and anxiety disorder. The best method of treatment is to treat both of these disorders at the same time. Typically methods of treatment that work with uncomplicated PTSD work in this circumstance as well.

How to Cope With PTSD Using Your Breath

While it might be difficult to get your life back on track if you have suffered PTSD, it is possible with short-term and long-term treatment options. These treatment options include medications and psychotherapy. While medication might be useful in treating the more extreme emotional and mental symptoms such as depression and emotional outbursts, psychotherapy helps teach the person how to deal with the symptoms. Implementing practical exercises learned here will help restore their self-esteem and self-confidence in dealing with everyday situations.

One of the long-term strategies that you can use, which is safe, natural, and effective is, of course, breathwork. Here are breathing techniques you can employ to help with PTSD symptoms.

Soft Focus Breathing

This breathing technique helps control the fight-or-flight response, which is easily triggered in a person with PTSD. To practice this technique, ensure that you are comfortable and sit cross-legged on a soft mat, chair, or bed. Put your hands on your face with your hands facing upward. Close your eyes and breathe in deeply and slowly through your nose. Allow the air to be guided to your diaphragm. Do this for a count on seven then release the air in a slow exhale through the mouth. Exhale for a count of seven so that you have balanced oxygen intake and carbon dioxide release. As you inhale, mentally project the image of softness to yourself. This can be an image of a cloud, a pillow, or any other object that you associate with softness. This will help direct your mind to a safe space and hence help you relax. This aids in dealing with the emotional and mental turmoil of PTSD symptoms. When you exhale, envision that whatever tension that you carry in your body and mind is being swallowed up by the softness. Do this for 5 minutes two to three times a day or as needed to help you relax. It can be done at bedtime to help you fall asleep faster.

7-11 breathing technique

This technique aids in lowering stress levels and promoting a calm state of mind. It is also as easy as the name suggests. You breathe in for a count of seven and exhale for a count of eleven. Ensure that your inhales go through your diaphragm and that your exhales are pushed out through pursed lips. This technique helps in the controlled release of carbon dioxide and to boost mental function for increased focus and clarity.

Active Breathing

This breathing technique is great for expelling fear, quieting the negative thoughts in your mind with breathwork as well as adjusting your mindset. Start in a standing position with a straight spin and arms at your side. Inhale deeply and slowly for a count of eight. Exhale for a count of eight as well but make a *shhh* sound when you do this. As you make this sounds, imagine that the thoughts in your head are people and that they respond to this sound by being quiet. The sound is also useful in opening up the diagram, which can close up when fear, anxiety, and stress are being felt. This limits the air volume that is taken into the body and so normal body and mental function.

Calming Breathing

In a standing position with your arms at your side and your spine straight, inhale through your nose for a count of seven. Allow the air to go to your diagram. Exhale through your nose and make an mmm sound as the air leaves your nostrils. Keep your lips closed to build the pressure so that the sound causes a vibration through your head. The vibration stimulates a nerve called the vagus nerve, which is located in the main branch of the parasympathetic nervous system. The vagus nerve happens to be the longest in the body and connects the brain to many important organs. It influences your breathing, digestive function, and more. Therefore, stimulating the vagus nerve allows the over-aroused nervous system to relax so that the PTSD patient can have improved clarity of thought and focus among its many benefits.

Other Meditation Practices for Trauma Therapy

The mind-body technique of meditation can also aid in relieving the symptoms of PTSD. The symptoms of PTSD such as flashbacks, anxiety, anger, mental confusion, and more are a bid the mind makes to ensure the survival of the individual involved. The mind floods the entire system of that human beings with sensations, images, emotions, and perceptions meant to keep that person alive. Therefore, meditation is a great way of refocusing that mental energy into a daily function rather than focusing on survival. Meditation encourages mental calm and self-awareness so that the person can move past the thoughts and feelings in their head to a better understanding of why their mind and body are reacting the way they are. It is only then that this person can employ strategies to help them cope and move past the trauma. Here are a few meditation exercises you can use to cope with the symptoms of PTSD.

Mindful Meditation for PTSD

The unpleasant thoughts and feelings that are associated with PTSD can distract from living in the moment. This takes away a person's joy and fulfillment and diverts it from where it should be, which is in the present and not in the past. Practicing mindful meditation can help get that person back in touch with the present as well as reduce the control that these unpleasant thoughts and feelings have on them. Mindful meditation also reduces stress and anxiety, both of which are conditions that are related to PTSD. The same routine in *Chapter 3: Meditation to Reduce Anxiety: A Simple Mindful Meditation Exercise* can be used and is just as effective in this instance.

Progressive Muscle Relaxation for PTSD

Our muscles natural tense in preparation for fight-or-flight mode when we are stressed and anxiety as like with PTSD suffering. Actively getting your muscles to relax can help alleviate the PTSD symptoms. To do this, get to a standing position. Ensure that your spine is straight. This technique relies on tensing up various parts of your body, then releasing that tension. Begin by inhaling for a count of eight. Ensure that the breath goes to your diaphragm. Hold the tension in your entire body for the inhale then let it go as you exhale for a count of eight. Exhale through pursed lips. Next, breathe and tense, then relax specific parts of your body. Start with your neck and throat. Next, perform the procedure on your shoulders, hands, and arms. The belly comes next then the leg and feet. Repeat the breathing process on each body area twice. When you exhale, imagine the tenseness melting off you like butter that has been heated. Finally, after you have performed the procedure over your entire body, continue breathing in and out for counts of eight, five more times. Sway from side to side as you do this so that you expel any lingering tension

Bamboo Swaying

This is also a meditative practice that is great for releasing muscle tension. Standing still with spine straight and your hands on your thighs in front of you, breathe in through your nose and out through pursed lips deeply and slowly. As you breathe, allow your chin to move forward until your upper body is bent enough to create an arch in your back. Pause there and exhale slowly for a count of eight. Allow your head to fall back and bring your tailbone forward slowly. Round your back and slowly return to an upright position. Repeat this three more times then begin to sway like a bamboo plant in a gentle breeze. Do this slowly and gently to dispel any tension that you are carrying. Pay attention to the movement and feeling in your spine.

Grounded Meditation

This practice is useful for expelling negative emotions and energy. It is an imaginary based exercise and starts with the practitioner standing straight with a straight spine and arms at the side. Keep your eyes open but allow them to defocus so that you are not really looking at anything. As you breathe in through your nose and out through pursed lips slowly and deeply, rise onto your toes then let yourself fall back down to your heels. Imagine that the entire weight drops down when your heels touch the floor. Imagine that this has a heavy sound and picture your negative emotions falling away with that weight. Keep repeating that rise and fall slowly as you breathe naturally and rhythmically. Continue this process for 1 minute.

The end... almost!

Reviews are not easy to come by.

As an independent author with a tiny marketing budget, I rely on readers, like you, to leave a short review on Amazon.

Even if it's just a sentence or two!

So if you enjoyed the book, please...

>> Click here to leave a brief review on Amazon.

https://www.amazon.com/review/create-review?asin=B087V78F63

I am very appreciative for your review as it truly makes a difference.

Thank you from the bottom of my heart for purchasing this book and reading it to the end.

Conclusion

You can change your life completely with your next breath.

These chapters were meant to show you that breathing is more than just a series of inhales and exhales but a more in-depth process that connects you with everything in the universe. This book was meant to show you that you can connect with yourself on the deepest and most fundamental level with a simple practice. It was meant to show you that this essential act that you do to keep on living does not just have to mean an existence but instead should mean that you can live happily, fulfilled and with reduced levels of anxiety, stress, and pain. My hope is that since you are reading this page that all of this and more has been accomplished.

Breathing with conscious, deliberate intent can transform your life instantly, and all it takes is that awareness that the process is happening, you can control it and the benefits that you reap from it. Many people think that conscious breathing is hippie nonsense but from the dawn of time, our ancestors saw the preciousness of it and incorporated it into so many of the best rejuvenating and healing practices we still use today. You too can be rejuvenated and healed with the power of breath starting today.

This might seem like a daunting task to accomplish all of this (the management of conditions like PTSD, anxiety disorders, chronic pain, etc.) through such simple means but do not be intimidated or uncertain. Many have accomplished great things as soon as they realized the power breathing has on their bodies, minds, hearts, and spirits. They realized the control they could exert over their entire beings. If they can do it, you can too. All it takes is that first conscious breath. Nothing is stopping you from reaping the benefits that breathwork has to offer except you.

One Last Thing...

I want to take this opportunity to thank you for downloading this book and wish you the best of luck in getting your breath and life under control.

DOWNLOAD YOUR FREE GIFT BELOW:

Go from Stress to Success with These 15 Powerful Tips

You're in The Tunnel, Now Turn on The Light:

Here are The Best Ways to Transform Your Success

Do You Feel Stressed-Out, Overwhelmed and Harassed Every Day?

Then you're stuck in a negative thought spiral that is keeping you from achieving *real success!*

How many times have you thought, 'if only I could be more productive, then I'd get ahead?' No matter how hard you try, it eludes you. Most people experience intense self-doubt, worry and negative thinking at some point in their careers. These are your immediate obstacles to success.

This guide tackles these issues with easy, direct solutions to help you break the cycle and get back on track. These 15 powerful tips will take you from overwhelmed to overjoyed, in no time!

This FREE Cheat Sheet contains:

- Essential tips on how to stop worrying and start living

- How to actually relieve anxiety and banish it for good

- Ways to get rid of negative thoughts, and how to stop them from recurring

- Tips to become the most productive, motivated version of yourself

- How to focus on career success and build positive cycles and habits

Scroll down and click the link **below to Claim your Free Cheat Sheet!**

I want you to know that you don't have to live this way. You don't have to feel like these negative cycles are getting the better of you. Your career is waiting to bloom – and flourish! Give yourself the opportunity to make the right choices, by learning how to authentically reach for lasting success.

Ditch the stress, embrace success.

Click Here!

Check out our Other *AMAZING* Titles:

Book 1: Dealing With Dementia and Alzheimer's

Your Guide to Coping With and Caring for a Loved One

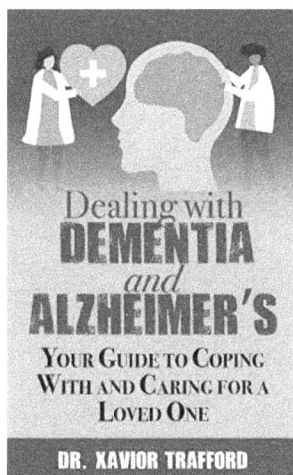

While early stage dementia and Alzheimer's patients can be taken care of at home or with a family member, as the disease progresses, it becomes more and more difficult to provide them with good quality of life. A large part of this is due to the fact that the moments of lucidity your loved one will have will result in them becoming aware of their state.

This will result in anger and a lot of negativity. Mood swings when directed at someone who is the primary caregiver will also leave the latter feeling helpless and angry. All in all, it is a very tough situation.

While end of life care is best provided by a facility, it is the middle stage that is the most difficult. There are a number of services which can reduce the load on your shoulders. This chapter is going to walk you through all the options you have available and also give you some tips on how you can choose the best services.

Adult Day Care

These centers will probably be your first stop before switching your loved one to a full-time facility. The fact is that being a caregiver to someone with dementia is exhausting and it is almost unmanageable if you have a full-time job to attend to as well. Adult day care centers exist to give caregivers a break and also help your loved one socialize with other people.

There are different types of daycare centers and their costs will vary depending on the services they offer. Almost every center will allow you to trial them for a short period. during this time, make sure your loved one is comfortable over there. These centers offer a number of services which include:

- Counseling - You will receive information about resources to help you or your loved one out.
- Medical tests - Some centers are equipped with staff that can carry out tests on your loved one and also check for any skin, dental, or foot problems.

- Dietary advice - Every good center will make a balanced and nutritious diet a priority. You won't have to worry about the food your loved one is going to receive.
- Behavior treatment - Your loved one may exhibit inappropriate behavior such as sudden anger or sexually inappropriate commentary. Most centers' staff are trained to handle such situations.
- Special needs - Daycare centers are usually equipped with special equipment your loved one might need like wheelchairs or medicine and so on.

Finding and Selecting

The best way of finding adult daycare centers is to refer to the Alzheimer's Association's local chapter. In addition to this, churches and senior care centers will also be able to refer you to reliable places. Once you've selected a few potential ones, consider their facilities and visit them in person.

Take your loved one along with you if this is possible and have them interact with people in the center and notice how the staff responds to them. The best way to get to know a center is to ask a lot of questions and to notice the patience with which people respond to your answers. Enquire about the trial period that they offer and if you find that there is no such period, ask about the minimum attendance requirements.

For a month, use the facility around twice or three times a week to get a feel for how they work and whether your loved one is adjusting well. You will need around a month because your loved one will need time to get used to their new environment. A major plus point for any center is the availability of transport.

A critical point to check up on is the training the staff have when it comes to dementia issues. Enquire whether the center evaluates their patients' medical care needs and if so, how often this is done. The qualifications of healthcare professionals working at the center should also be checked out.

Costs are a major factor in your decision. Check if your insurance or Mediclaim will cover your expenses. In some states, Medicaid covers expenses for families with low income. Take note that some centers organize field trips and these usually involve additional expense.

Prior to enrolling your loved one into the center, make sure to update the staff about any specific issues. Wandering is a major issue in three out of five AD patients, which concerns wandering away from a place in confusion ("Stages and Behaviors," 2019). So, if the center brings these points up proactively, it's a good sign they're reliable.

Assisted Living

Assisted living is a step above a daycare center but isn't a facility that has full medical assistance. If your loved one is having trouble completing daily tasks such as dressing themselves or eating and such, assisted living facilities are a great option. There are some factors you ought to consider before moving them into a facility like this, so let's take a look at them one by one.

Safety

This is the number one reason people choose assisted living. As much as you can try, it is impossible to predict how your loved one is going to interact with the things in your home and use it to unknowingly harm themselves. Flights of stairs, light fixtures, and so on are hazards that are impossible to completely remove.

Assisted living facilities will usually have staff on site to monitor their movements and also bring meals to them so you won't have to worry about nutrition or any other concerns. The facility environment will also encourage your loved one to be more social and interact with other people.

Your Loved One's Health

The health of your loved one determines whether you need to seek a facility that can offer more specialized care or one which is a little less on the medical scale and focuses exclusively on assistance with living. Check with your doctor prior to making any decision.

If your loved one is susceptible to infection or has a history of some other disease, a facility fully equipped with medical aid will be more suited to their needs.

Behavior

If you're struggling to cope with your loved one's moodiness and if the outbursts seem to be increasing, consider the fact that there might be too many triggers in the environment around your home. When this happens, a change of scenery is the best choice for everyone involved and assisted living facilities provide this.

You do need to check the qualifications of the staff at the facility and check whether they are qualified to handle your loved one's behavior. Generally, staff at such places are well trained and the facility is equipped to handle behavior of this kind. Wandering is the biggest problem, so check to see if the facility has provisions to handle this.

You

Last but not least, you need to consider the burden you're currently undertaking and whether you're able to provide the best quality care to your loved one. You will feel guilty about moving them into a facility but remember that a tired and stressed out caregiver is the last thing your loved one needs.

You do have a life to live and you cannot function properly in any aspect of life if you're stressed out all the time. This is not an easy decision to make, so take your time with it but don't delay it by too much. Reach out to support organizations such as your local parish or any other organizations you can interact with.

Take a tour of these facilities and check their references thoroughly. Your doctor will also have some suggestions in this regard so take note of that. This is not an easy decision to make and before doing so involve all of the caregivers in your family and seek their input prior to making one.

Home Care

The early stages of Alzheimer's often sees patients living with their families or even by themselves before their condition deteriorates. Some families choose to continue with the home care option despite increasing inconvenience. Such families tend to be either very wealthy or come from the lower income brackets. Either way, remember that unless you can afford close to full time medical assistance within your home, a facility is the best place for your loved one.

Use the guidelines in the previous section to figure out when the time comes to make the switch. Despite your loved one's condition being manageable initially, you should not confuse this with it being an easy situation. Caring for someone with dementia and AD is stressful and will place huge burdens on your relationships and existing family bonds.

I'll talk about the emotional demands more in the following chapter, but for now, follow these tips to make your home as safe as possible for your loved one.

AD Proof Your Home

Follow the tips mentioned in an earlier chapter about the steps you need to take to make sure your home is as safe as it can possibly be. Your loved one is still going to have a lot of capacity initially so take their input into consideration.

The biggest risk you'll have to deal with is the tendency of those with AD to wander. So, make your home as wander proof as possible. Depending on the type of dementia your loved one is experiencing, you'll have to deal with different scenarios and this requires a lot of empathy on your part.

Empathy

Imagine if you woke up disoriented and unsure of where you were or who you were. This is what your loved one is going through, so be patient with them and strive to be as understanding as possible. At times, it will be infuriating for you, but understand that they're not doing this on purpose.

Compounding this problem will be your own sense of helplessness. There is nothing you can do except wait and watch and this understandably gets to people. If your loved one experiences a personality change, as is common in some forms of dementia, you will begin to wonder if it's even worth taking care of this person since they're so different from the person you love.

Reach out for support and keep educating yourself all the time. This is the best way of dealing with things. Never isolate yourself or your loved one under any circumstances.

Plan

You need to be strong and plan for the future. You will need to move them into a facility at some point and you will need extra assistance along the way. All of this requires planning with the rest of your family and you'll need to take costs into consideration.

As painful as it is to deal with all of this, the situation will not get better if you ignore it. So, deal with it as best as you can and do your best. A good idea to consider is signing up for home care services. There are all kinds of services available and if you're uncomfortable moving your loved one into a daycare or a full-time facility, these options will reduce your burden greatly.

Home Care Services

There are a number of services you can opt for when it comes to a home care service. Some of these are:

- Companion services - For recreational activities, visiting, or other forms of supervision.
- Personal care - Things such as cooking, bathing, and so on.

- Housekeeping - As the name suggests, performing daily chores and taking care of your home.
- Medical care - Assistance providers will be trained in making sure their patients are taking their medication and can even administer them.

Finding Services

The best place to start is to ask your doctor or utilize Medicare's Home Health Compare tool. This will give you a list of Medicare qualified professionals in your area. Look specifically for people who are qualified and have experience caring for people with dementia. The Alzheimer's Association website has a number of tools which make it easier to narrow down both what you should look for in a service provider as well as resources to help you find someone qualified.

Another option is to ask family and friends for someone they recommend. Reach out to as many people as possible to select the best person for the job.

Choose

Before choosing a provider, sit down and make a list of all the services you need along with your expectations of the service that needs to be provided. You have a choice of choosing between an agency and an individual provider. Both have their advantages. People coming from an agency can be held to higher accountability standards.

If something goes wrong, you know there's at least someone to complain to. Individual providers tend to be more experienced and add a personal touch to things. Most of the time, individual providers prove to be a better fit but it can be tough to find someone who is reliable. Weigh both options accordingly.

Before meeting them in person, call ahead and check to see if they're okay with providing the services you need. Once this is done, schedule an interview and aside from reviewing their qualifications, check to see if they're a good fit with your loved one. Admittedly, it is tough to figure this out in just a single meeting but engage them in a dialogue to see how they would handle the issues you need help with.

At a minimum, check for the following things:

- Do they provide backup in case of sickness or some other issue? How qualified is the backup?
- Their references.
- Are they trained in basic first aid procedures and others like CPR?
- What time are they available? How should they be contacted?
- Are they bonded? This protects you from any losses caused by them while taking care of your loved one.
- Their training and other relevant information.

The costs of in-home care services vary depending on the type of service provided. Most services are covered by Medicare provided the nature of the service passes certain criteria ("Stages and Behaviors," 2019). In addition to this, there are a few cash assistance programs which provide financial assistance to seniors who need it. You can find these using the Eldercare website at https://www.eldercare.gov.

Memory Care

Memory care units are additions to assisted living facilities with a particular focus on patients suffering from dementia or Alzheimer's. These facilities are a bit more expensive than your usual assisted living units. On average, assisted living costs around $3-4000 per month in

America while the average memory care facility costs around $7000 (Sauer, 2018).

Given the cost, it is valid to ask what you're receiving in return. Well, memory care facilities have specially trained staff and have facilities designed to make them safe for people suffering from dementia. So, things like locks and latches are designed in a way to prevent wandering.

Finding a good memory care center is a tough task. This is because "good" in this context needs to provide value for money as well. The truth is that there is a trend of a lot of these centers promising more than what they deliver. A few facilities end up resembling jails thanks to their emphasis on preventing wandering and you need to thoroughly inspect and research the institution before moving your loved one there.

The best way to do this, over and above the same steps as outlined in the assisted living section, is to visit the place during unscheduled times and check to see how the staff respond. Often these places have differently qualified staff on different shifts so your loved one might end up under the care of someone from the wider assisted living pool.

On the plus side, this type of care is far more comprehensive. The safer environment provides greater encouragement to the patients and promotes more freedom if done right. Furthermore, a lot of facilities offer therapeutic programs to specifically slow down the effects of dementia and social activities geared towards those suffering from it.

The higher quality of life this results in not only improves the lives of the patients but will also provide you with the peace of mind that your loved one is in good hands. As always, do your research thoroughly before choosing a facility. Always check their references and speak to doctors in the area to get a feel for what the facility is like.

Pay attention to any complaints or lawsuits you might happen to come across. You obviously want to stay away from a place that has been hit with a lawsuit.

Continuing Care Communities

Continuing care communities is a broad umbrella term and there are a lot of different types of facilities that come underneath it. Memory care units and assisted living facilities are two types of such communities. For those who need greater assistance, nursing homes offer around the clock care and personalized facilities depending on the type of facility.

A lot of nursing homes have dedicated Alzheimer's units which are well-equipped to take care of your loved one's needs. One thing to watch out for is whether these units are housed separately from the rest of the facility or is integrated. Neither option is better than the other but you do want to check the rationale behind such a design.

This is due to the fact that you don't want your loved one to become isolated during their time there. So, check the references of the nursing home thoroughly and also check their accreditations. Nursing home contracts can be arcane so it is worth it to run these past a lawyer to check for any irregularities.

Some nursing homes have strict meal times and this can be an inconvenience. So, check all the rules and regulations to minimize any discomfort that might occur. A good idea is to network with social workers in your area to get inside information on the nursing home. In addition to this, check the place out for how well they provide a safe space in open air for your loved one.

Once you've moved your loved one into the new place, check in regularly to see if they're being well taken care of. Do not hesitate to raise any issues you might find. Monitor your loved one for their weight or any other health issues they might be suffering from. Monitoring weight and their overall state of hygiene and cleanliness is very important to since these are the major indicators of how well the facility provides care.

All in all, choosing an assisted living option is a very tough choice and is a deeply emotional one. You may feel guilty about doing this and will want to keep your loved one under your care for as long as possible, but remember that their quality of life comes before your emotional needs.

So, always make the best decision for them. It may not be easy but it is for the best. Do not delay transferring them to an assisted facility since prolonging this increases the risk of an accident or them contracting a disease thanks to less than ideal care. Take your time and plan the options available to you when your loved one is under your care.

This will help you prepare for the future better. As you can see there is a lot of responsibility on your shoulders and it will be overwhelming at times. As important as it is to take care of your loved one, you matter as well. Learning to take care of yourself during this time is essential, and that is what the next chapter is all about.

Book 2: Anxiety and Panic Attacks

A Guide to Overcoming Severe Anxiety, Controlling Panic Attacks and Reclaiming Your Life Again

DR. HERMAN KYNASTON

ANXIETY
AND
PANIC ATTACKS
A GUIDE TO OVERCOMING SEVERE ANXIETY

CONTROLLING PANIC
ATTACKS AND RECLAIMING YOUR LIFE AGAIN

Treatments and Therapies

Therapies for an anxiety disorder:

Cognitive behavior therapy:

One of the best ways to treat anxiety. Anxiety and panic attacks are a result of thinking about the future and what could be the disastrous implications of it. People are made aware that their thinking is what causes the physical symptoms in the first place, so it is better to stop right then and there. (C. Butler, E. Chapman & M.Forman, 2006)[1]

Exposure therapy:

As the name suggests, this therapy will make you confront the situation that you run away from due to their stress and anxiety-inducing effects. The idea is that through repeated, continued exposure, you can overcome the feeling of dread that settles upon you when facing those kinds of situations. Your sense of control over the particular situation will gradually increase.

There are also medications available for the treatment of anxiety and panic attacks.

Treatment for anxiety:

There is not one single test that is undertaken to prove that you could have anxiety. It is done through a long process of mental health evaluations, questionnaires, and physical exams. There are also tests and scales that will find out the level of anxiety a person has. To start off, on your first session, you will undergo a psychological evaluation. You will be asked about your feeling and thoughts.

Experiencing more than one condition at once is possible. Untreated anxiety will worsen over time. If left like that, to worsen, it will be more difficult to treat. It is difficult to distinguish between an anxiety disorder or a really bad day. However, these are some of the signs that you should absolutely not ignore and head out to seek help.

---

[1] C. Butler, A., E. Chapman, J., & M.Forman, E. (2006). The empirical status of cognitive-behavioral therapy: A review of meta-analyses [Ebook]. Science Direct.

- Your constant worry is affecting your everyday routine life. You feel as though you would be able to perform them more efficiently if not for the nagging thoughts of your brain.

- You have started relying on unhealthy coping mechanisms to escape from your own thoughts and fears.

- Once little worries and nagging thoughts have grown to genuinely distress you now to the point of having suicidal thoughts.

Once you have decided that it's time to seek help, then first comes the visit to a physician. It is to make sure that anxiety is not due to a physical condition. Once it's proved to not be a physical case, then you will be referred to mental health specialists.

A psychologist is a mental health professional who will use counseling only to treat mental health conditions. A psychiatrist is a licensed doctor who will treat mental health conditions through medications and other treatments. They are both able to diagnose a person.

Finding the right mental health care provider is very important. You should be able to feel comfortable in their presence enough to open up about yourself. If that is not the case, then there is no point in seeking therapy. If you are determined to go to proper therapy, then seek the right kind of help from the right person.

Treatment of anxiety yields its result gradually and you need to be patient to see them. Following the direction of your healthcare provider is the key to finding a long term cure for anxiety. Be sure to take your medications regularly and don't skip appointments. Following through both of these tasks will help keep your anxiety disorder symptoms at bay.

Treatment for anxiety is a 24/7 type of task. While treatments, medications, and counseling will yield positive results in due time, there are some simple lifestyle changes that you could acquire which will help in fighting off anxiety.

You must make efforts to know what triggers your anxiety. So consciously you can work around those symptoms and try to come up with a solution preferably better than avoiding it altogether. Your mental health care provider will help you with specific coping strategies against those triggers. So, next time you are prepared to deal with your anxiety.

Writing down your behaviors about certain experiences and situations will ultimately help your mental healthcare provider gain more insight into your condition. He will then make a more effective treatment plan for you based on that knowledge.

It is recommended to find a support group near you. Listening to them and talking with them throws a positive outlook on the whole scenario. It means you are not alone, That more people are facing the same issues. You will be more determined than before to continue your struggle against your anxiety.

Some people experiencing anxiety tend to shy away from friends and family. You must know that it will only make your anxiety way worse than before. Relying on people is an important step to take for people suffering from a mental disorder. You have to know that people are there to support you and they are not going to go anywhere. Distancing yourself from ones you love could lead to a more anxious feeling such as you constantly wondering what they are going to think of you. You will only end up making assumptions in your head that are far away from reality and they will end up hurting you more.

Effects and Types of Anxiety

Some of the effects that anxiety could have on our body besides the physical symptoms that manifest are:

- The cardiovascular system is seriously affected by constant worry and anxiety. Increased heartbeat and palpitations along with chest pains only spell trouble for you in the long run.

- Anxiety can also directly affect the digestive system. It can cause diarrhea or vomiting in case of extreme anxiety.

- If you frequently suffer from anxiety, then it can take a toll on your immune system as well. Adrenaline is released in your body whenever you experience a severe case of anxiety. It can boost your immune system for a little while, but over time, it will have bad effects on your immune system.

- Muscle fatigue and tension in the body are caused by experiencing anxiety and panic attacks.

Types of anxiety disorder:

Generalized Anxiety Disorder (GAD):

Generalized anxiety disorder is when even mundane daily activities can induce feelings of anxiety in a person. The situation doesn't call for that much stress as a person experiencing this disorder may feel. Stress and constant worry will cause adverse effects on a person's health. They may experience insomnia and upset stomach.

Obsessive Compulsive Disorder (OCD):

It is a mental disorder where there is a constant barrage of unwanted, intrusive thoughts. They will cause one to develop obsessive behaviors where they will do a certain thing over and over again. These compulsive behaviors will only provide a short term relief, but the person with the disorder will be doing them to get rid of intrusive thoughts in the first place.

Without performing these routines will result in a great deal of distress for the person, so they carry on with this behavior.

Agoraphobia:

People suffering from this disorder presume certain situations or places to be the cause of their stress. They experience mortification just by the thought of them. So, they try to avoid them as much as possible as it can lead to them having a panic attack.

Post-traumatic stress disorder (PTSD):

PTSD is usually caused after a very nightmarish situation.

Some disturbing experiences such as war, an assault, or an accident are some of the main causes of post-traumatic stress disorder. After a large scale natural disaster hits, one of the most mental disorder cases to arise is PTSD. Some of its symptoms are insomnia, nightmares, and flashbacks of troubled times.

Separation Anxiety Disorder:

It mainly occurs in younger children. This type of anxiety prevails when a child is separated from their parents. Most outgrow this anxiety around 18 months. It is a normal childhood condition. In some of the cases, children continue to depict versions of it that might become an issue as it causes a disturbance in their daily routine. For example, children refusing to perform well in school in the early years just because of this disorder.

Selective mutism:

Some children refuse to engage themselves when placed in specific situations or places. They outright don't talk. This disorder is called selective mutism and it can have a huge effect on daily routine and the person himself if not recognized and left untreated. An example is that they will not say a word at school but talk just fine at home.

Panic disorder:

Panic disorder is a frequent occurrence of panic attacks. They could be sudden or a result of a gradual buildup of anxiety.

Phobias:

Phobia is when a certain object, a specific situation or place can trigger severe anxiety in a person when they encounter it. They have a mighty need to avoid it at all costs. Some examples are claustrophobia (fear of being in cramped or small spaces) or coulrophobia (fear of clowns).

How to cope with anxiety

Nutrition and Anxiety

One might wonder whether what we eat can help us with our anxiety. Well, the answer is simple, yes. Depression and anxiety go hand in hand. If you set out to cure one of them, it will indirectly cure the other one as well.

Complex carbohydrates are metabolized relatively slowly. So, it means that blood sugar levels will not be spiking and it will help keep the body relax.

Skipping meals is a big no-no. When you are dealing with anxiety disorder especially, it all becomes a game of blood sugar level. Fluctuating blood sugar levels are directly related to mood swings.

The standard American diet cannot directly cause anxiety, but it can definitely make it worse. As it is full of sugar and fat, it is not very good for your physical health as well. A random sugar high and crash will cause shaking and tension in the body. It will severely impair a body's ability to deal with stress.

Anxiety relieving diet

- Try food rich in magnesium. They include Spanish, legumes, nuts, and seeds.

- Oysters, liver, beef and egg yolks should be included in the diet as they are rich in zinc. They are proven to be helpful in reducing anxiety.

- Omega-3s help improve depression and anxiety both. Their main source is salmon.

- Avocados and almonds are foods enriched in vitamin B.

- Those 'feel good' foods that release neurotransmitters such as dopamine and serotonin are safe.

- Try to take foods enriched in antioxidants. A lowered antioxidant state is thought to be correlated to anxiety. Some foods enriched in antioxidants are beans, pecans, fruits, and berries. Especially turmeric and ginger have both antioxidant and anti-anxiety properties.

Random spikes in blood sugar levels will cause moody behavior and depression. Try to eat regularly, so you avoid feeling negative altogether. Neglecting your personal needs could not only physically drain you but could be exponentially bad for your mental health especially if you suffer from anxiety disorder.

Natural remedies for anxiety:

Exercise, meditation, and yoga are excellent techniques and they are discussed further in detail in upcoming chapters.

Some other natural remedies are:

Acupuncture is the ancient Chinese medical practice of inserting very thin needles at certain points of the body. It is believed to be effective in fighting off anxiety.

Kava is a herb that comes from a crushed root of a Polynesian shrub. Some studies have proved that it helps in the treatment of anxiety although there is not definite proof. It is still a natural thing and has no adverse side effects when taken into moderation.

Lavender is believed to have a calming and soothing scent. It is used for aromatherapy. It can help soothe frayed nerves, but it doesn't actually treat the disorder itself.

Breathing exercise: it is better to keep your eyes closed. Shutting down your vision could relieve your brain from so much activity and it will also help in tune your other senses.

- First of all, inhale through the nose slowly and gently. Try to take as much a deep breath as you can.

- Exhale through the mouth just as you inhaled, slowly and deeply.

It is also a good technique to count to a number. It just helps focus on your breathing more.

"Nothing can bring you peace but yourself."

Ralph Waldo Emerson

Dealing with Anxiety Everyday

Doing breathing exercises will help you become more confident in your ability to fend off panic attacks.

Exercise and a well-balanced diet could do wonders to improve mood. Once your lifestyle is positive, then your thoughts start to become positive as well. You have to make that choice though.

Caffeine alcohol and smoking make the panic and anxiety disorders worse so try to stay away from those as much as possible. Make better health choices. (Connolly, 2018)[2]

Yoga, meditation are some of the relaxation and stress management techniques that will put your mind at peace. They are ultimately related to positive attitude and will greatly prove beneficial to people experiencing an anxiety disorder.

Getting a good night sleep and eating at appropriate times are the simplest things that you can easily embed into your life. They will yield incredibly positive results in your life and make it much more productive and smoother.

Living and coping with anxiety is no piece of cake. It drains your energy that you would much rather put in something productive. However, it is no use to hide from anxiety. You must accept it at one stage and learn to deal with it. If you remain determined and preserved, then you can eventually overcome it as well. There are some simple steps you can take to better deal with anxiety.

Try to collect as much information as you can about your condition. Don't hesitate to ask your doctor as well. Don't shy away from making healthy choices for your life. Some people may call them old style as compared to this haphazard lifestyle which is very common now. Today's lifestyle of being blinded by the success of money and fame could lead to detrimental effects on one's mental wellbeing.

---

[2] Connolly, M. (2018). Anxiety and Caffeine - this stimulant in coffee or tea may fuel anxiety. Retrieved from https://www.psycom.net/anxiety-and-caffeine

Book 3: Chakra for Beginners:

A Self Help Guide: Transform your Life with Chakras, Spiritual Awakening and Energy Healing

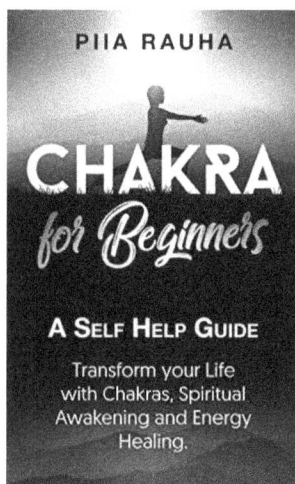

This guidebook has spent a good deal of time looking at what the chakras are all about as well as some of the different activities that you are able to work on, to take care of those chakras. In this chapter, we are going to spend a little more time taking a look at some of the other things that you can do to help strengthen the chakras and make them feel better than ever before.

Visualization

Visualization is another great technique that you can try out to work on the chakras. We talked about a version of visualization earlier on when we talked about doing meditation while thinking about the different colors of the chakras, but that is just one of the many ways that you can work on visualization. For those who are having some issues with working on meditation or who need to have something to work on while they are doing the deep breathing exercises, visualization is the choice that you should go with.

When it comes to working with visualization, you are going to spend about ten or fifteen minutes each day focusing on a picture of your choice.

With this exercise, we are going to imagine what it feels like to be on the beach. This is a popular choice for a lot of people when it comes to visualization because a beach is seen as relaxing and can help to calm them down at the end of a hard day. To get started with this exercise, you will want to find a quiet place where you are able to be all alone for a little bit, just like you did when working on meditation.

You want to make sure that the heart rate is pretty steady and ready to go before you go into this activity, or you may rush through it. You can also consider setting a timer for the fifteen minutes if you need to get somewhere, so you don't have to worry about watching the clock.

Once the breathing has slowed down a little bit and you feel comfortable, it is time to work on the visualization a bit. Some people may see the beach as empty so that they get the whole place to themselves, while others will see other kids and families wandering around and enjoying the day as well. Who is there with you? What are some of the sights and the smells that you encounter? Where would be the best place for you to set up a camp so that you can relax?

While you are on the beach, you will want to make sure that you are touching things and getting some of the sensations as well. How does the hot sand feel on your feet and in your hands as you play with it? How do the seashells sound, as you pick them up off the ground? Does the cold water of the ocean feel good, or how about that nice cool drink when you are trying to relax?

There are so many things that you can imagine when you think about the beach scene and you are going to want to take your time to go through it as much as possible. Experience that beach scene and enjoy it as much as possible in that time frame. There is no hurry and there is no limit on what you can experience. If you spend the whole time watching the waves and feeling the cool water lap against your toes, that is just fine. You just imagine things in a nice slow pace during that time frame.

When the time is up, you will do a few more slow breaths before heading back to whatever you needed to get done with during the day. You are able to come back to this scene each day, exploring the things that you liked the most or trying out something new each day to have some fun. You can also change out the scenes that you would like to work with, maybe switching it out with spending time with your kids or having the time to work on your chakras. The choice is up to you but giving yourself some of this time each day to relax and to enjoy the sights and sounds that you would like can help to align the chakras and will ensure that your stress levels are going down as well.

Yoga

Yoga is often one of the preferred methods for helping you to align your chakras. This is often practiced in many of the spiritual schools of thought and the religions that recognize the chakras and can be really effective, as well as being a great stretch for the whole body. You have a lot of freedom with the type of yoga that you do. While some poses seem to work the best for specific chakras, there is also a lot of variety and you are able to pick out the poses that work the best for you. If you are a beginner with yoga, keep in mind that you can make modifications to the moves and then increase the intensity as you get a bit stronger. You can find some of the moves that you would like to use online or stick with a guided program to help you learn how to do things the right way.

Gemstones

Some people choose to work with gemstones to help their chakras work properly. The idea with this one is that you will need to pick out the gemstone that is right for the chakra that you want to heal. So, if you would like to work with the heart chakra, you would use a green gemstone and then if you would like to work on the crown chakra, you would need a violet one and so on. This can be effective for healing the chakras as long as you use the right colors.

Essential Oils

One method that a lot of people like to work with to clear out their chakras includes essential oils. These oils are so amazing for the whole body and since they are all natural and there are so many different kinds, you are going to be amazed at how well they work and how many different ailments they can help out with. If you have ever been curious about working with your chakras, it is time to bring in some essential oils.

The method that most people are going to stick with includes taking a bath in the essential oil. This will allow you to reach total relaxation while getting to have the essential oil work on your skin and through your nose.

The important part is to learn more about the chakras and then focus some of your energy on them to make yourself feel better. You can choose any of these methods that you would like, and sometimes you may have to work with a few of them to get the best results.

References

Bisson, J. I., Cosgrove, S., Lewis, C., & Robert, N. P. (2015). Post-traumatic stress disorder. *BMJ (Clinical research ed.), 351*, h6161. doi:10.1136/bmj.h6161

Bandelow, B., & Michaelis, S. (2015). Epidemiology of anxiety disorders in the 21st century. *Dialogues in clinical neuroscience, 17*(3), 327–335.

Bandelow, B., Michaelis, S., & Wedekind, D. (2017). Treatment of anxiety disorders. *Dialogues in clinical neuroscience, 19*(2), 93–107.

Chipidza, F., Wallwork, R. S., Adams, T. N., & Stern, T. A. (2016). Evaluation and Treatment of the Angry Patient. The primary care companion for CNS disorders, 18(3), 10.4088/PCC.16f01951. doi:10.4088/PCC.16f01951

Cho, H., Ryu, S., Noh, J., & Lee, J. (2016). The Effectiveness of Daily Mindful Breathing Practices on Test Anxiety of Students. *PloS one, 11(*10), e0164822. doi:10.1371/journal.pone.0164822

Crofford L. J. (2015). Chronic Pain: Where the Body Meets the Brain. *Transactions of the American Clinical and Climatological Association, 126*, 167–183.

Gerritsen, R., & Band, G. (2018). Breath of Life: The Respiratory Vagal Stimulation Model of Contemplative Activity. *Frontiers in human neuroscience, 12*, 397. doi:10.3389/fnhum.2018.00397

Hilton, L., Hempel, S., Ewing, B. A., Apaydin, E., Xenakis, L., Newberry, S., … Maglione, M. A. (2017). Mindfulness Meditation for Chronic Pain: Systematic Review and Meta-analysis. *Annals of behavioral medicine : a publication of the Society of Behavioral Medicine, 51*(2), 199–213. doi:10.1007/s12160-016-9844-2

Russo, M. A., Santarelli, D. M., & O'Rourke, D. (2017). The physiological effects of slow breathing in the healthy human. *Breathe (Sheffield, England), 13*(4), 298–309. doi:10.1183/20734735.009817

Sheng, J., Liu, S., Wang, Y., Cui, R., & Zhang, X. (2017). The Link between Depression and Chronic Pain: Neural Mechanisms in the Brain. *Neural plasticity, 2017*, 9724371. doi:10.1155/2017/9724371

Walker, J., 3rd, & Pacik, D. (2017). Controlled Rhythmic Yogic Breathing as Complementary Treatment for Post-Traumatic Stress Disorder in Military Veterans: A Case Series. *Medical acupuncture, 29*(4), 232–238. doi:10.1089/acu.2017.1215

Williams R. (2017). Anger as a Basic Emotion and Its Role in Personality Building and Pathological Growth: The Neuroscientific, Developmental and Clinical Perspectives. Frontiers in psychology, 8, 1950. doi:10.3389/fpsyg.2017.01950

Zaccaro, A., Piarulli, A., Laurino, M., Garbella, E., Menicucci, D., Neri, B., & Gemignani, A. (2018). How Breath-Control Can Change Your Life: A Systematic Review on Psycho-Physiological Correlates of Slow Breathing. *Frontiers in human neuroscience, 12*, 353. doi:10.3389/fnhum.2018.00353

www.ingramcontent.com/pod-product-compliance
Lightning Source LLC
Chambersburg PA
CBHW030842090426
42737CB00009B/1077